Principles
of
Esoteric
Healing

Dion Fortune

edited, with an introduction by
Gareth Knight

Sun Chalice Books

Published by

Sun Chalice Books

PO Box 5355
Oceanside, CA
USA 92052

sunchalice@earthlink.net
www.magigroup.net/sunchalice

Copyright © 2000 The Society of the Inner Light
Introduction Copyright © 2000 Gareth Knight

All rights reserved. No part of this book may be reproduced or transmitted in any form without written permission from the publisher except for the inclusion of brief quotations in a review.

This book is a reference work based on the author's research. Any techniques and suggestions are used at the reader's sole discretion. The opinions expressed herein are not necessarily those of or endorsed by the publisher. The directions stated in this book are not intended as a substitute for consultation with a duly licensed doctor.

Publisher's Cataloging-in-publication Data

Fortune, Dion
     Principles of esoteric healing / Dion Fortune
       p.   cm.
     Includes index
     1. Healing
  2. Mental healing   I. Knight, Gareth   II. Title

   RZ401 .F00 2000   615.8/5 19

ISBN 1-928754-03-1

Book and cover design by Nicholoas Whitehead

Contents

INTRODUCTION
Gareth Knight: DION FORTUNE AND
THE MASTER OF MEDICINE 7

**1. THE ESOTERIC PHILOSOPHY OF
THE ART OF HEALING** 17
The Method of Approach 17
The Spiritual Principles of Healing 20
The Work and Essentials of a true Physician 23
The Scope of Esoteric medicine 25

2. ESOTERIC ANATOMY 27
The Development of the
Subtle Bodies in the Light of Evolution 27
The Doctrine of the Ghost 28
The Relationship of the
Subtle Bodies to Astrology 32
The Relationship between Man and the Universe 34
The Fourfold Constitution of Man 36

**3. THE CLASSIFICATION
OF DISEASES** 41
The Types of Disease 42
The Principles of Physical Disease 42
Diseases of the Etheric Double 46
Diseases of the Astral Plane 49
Diseases of the Mental Plane 53
Poisoning and Sepsis 52

4. ESOTERIC DIAGNOSIS 61
First Principles of Esoteric Diagnosis 61
Development of the Intuitive Faculty 66
Intuitional perception and the Higher Self 69

Development of the Clairvoyant Faculty 70
The Significance of the Etheric Double 72
Thought Forms 72
Practical Applications 74
Correspondences 75

5. THERAPEUTIC METHODS 79
Relaxation and its Value 79
Suggestion 81
Hypnosis 86
Vitality 91
Diathesis 92
Primary and Secondary Reactions
    in relation to Treatment 95
Insomnia 98
Meditation Sequence on the Temple
    of Asclepios-Apollo 102
The Use of Consecrated Oil
    in treating Etheric Leakage 103
Rapports: Obessession and Overshadowing
    – Origin and Treatment 105
Esoteric Hygiene and Anti-Sepsis 110

6. THE CENTRES 113
The Centres in the Four Worlds 115
The Centres in Diagnosis 134
General Principles of Treatment in the Four Worlds 140

7. THE ETHERIC DOUBLE 145
The Etheric Centres 145
The Etheric Double and the Endocrine Glands 148
Endocrine Malfunction 152
Principles concerning Conception and Birth 156
Astrological Factors 158

INDEX 161

INTRODUCTION

by Gareth Knight

DION FORTUNE AND THE MASTER OF MEDICINE

One of the most exciting recent literary finds in the archives of the Society of the Inner Light has been a bundle of files labelled "Esoteric Therapeutics". This had been assumed to be the work of a former member of the Society, a doctor of medicine, who saw long service with the Society from 1946 onwards but who is now deceased.

However, on studying the contents in detail, they were plainly written up from records of the mediumship of Dion Fortune, with a particular contact who was known to her as "the Master of Medicine". Some of this material goes back as far as 1921 and continues through to at least 1942.

The original intention of the communicator had been to write a book, even to found a school of esoteric medicine. For one reason and another the book was never published, the school never founded, although some of the teaching was privately circulated to suitably qualified individuals.There were in 1927/8 plans afoot to open a centre for esoteric healing at Dorking in Surrey, to the southwest of London.

Apart from any intrinsic value of the text itself, it is also of interest for the light it throws upon the life and work of Dion Fortune. It is indeed, on reflection, hardly surprising that she should have been responsible for a work of this nature, in

Principles of Esoteric Healing

that she had a para-medical and psychotherapeutic background to many stages of her life.

Her parents had been involved in running a hydro-therapeutic centre, and she herself, when still in her early twenties, developed a practical interest in psycho-analysis. She practised in 1915-16 as a therapist at the Medico-Psychological Clinic, an organisation set up to treat by medical and psychological means functional nervous diseases and disorders accompanying organic diseases, and to extend in the community a knowledge of the laws of mental hygiene. She even gave public lectures on psychology that were collected and published in volume form as *The Machinery of the Mind*. They may seem dated today but at the time were thought worthy to be graced with a sympathetic foreword by a distinguished scientist, A.G.Tansley F.R.S..

It was from this background that she gradually moved towards more fully committed esoteric interests, and the series of stories she wrote for the *Royal Magazine* in the early 1920's, "The Secrets of Dr. Taverner," had as their protagonist an occultly informed medical practitioner.

The role model for Dr. Taverner is said to be, from evidence of her own remarks, a charismatic occult teacher under whom she studied, Dr. Theodore Moriarty. It should be said that he was not a medical practitioner, nor did he ever run a private nursing home, but he gave esoteric teaching, sometimes on residential courses, and in this respect served as a convenient hook upon which to hang a character sketch for her hero.

A strong medical link developed in 1925 in the form of Dr. Thomas Penry Evans, who with his sister, a nurse, lodged at Dion Fortune's newly acquired London headquarters in Bayswater. Their relationship blossomed, and on 7th April 1927 they were married. The most important and consistent contacts with the Master of Medicine date from the beginning of August 1927, a few months after this event.

Dion Fortune and the Master of Medicine

There had been one or two passing contacts with this source in 1921 when Dion Fortune was developing her mediumistic capacity with her friend and mentor in the Alpha et Omega Temple of the former Hermetic Order of the Golden Dawn, Maiya Curtis-Webb, who was married to a doctor, and later, as Maiya Tranchell-Hayes, to a leading psychiatrist

In the earliest of these sessions to have survived in manuscipt, on 11th January 1921, we find a quantity of medically related communication suddenly coming through. There is no named identity recorded, and the content is somewhat disjointed and even garbled. Indeed, it might be viewed as apprentice work on the part of both medium and communicator — although the transcription skills of the scribe, who is unlikely to have had shorthand, is another unknown factor.

The communication seems to start in full spate, and goes on somewhat breathlessly about the possible effect of the ductless glands (the endocrine system) in dementia praecox (now generally known as schizophrenia) and how hypnotic suggestion might be used in relation to both. The general theme is that the emotions, or the lower astral plane, can be the cause of physical disease by acting through the etheric vehicle. The importance of the seven planes is also stressed, and their influence one upon the other, from spiritual through to the physical level.

This seems to be part of a series of more or less fortnightly meetings during the early part of 1921. The subject matter veers off onto more general occult themes but later returns to medical topics. Emphasis is laid on the need to distinguish between two major types of disease. On the one hand those that are genuinely physical in origin, and which act from below upwards; and on the other hand those which have an inner causation, and act from above to below in terms of the planes of consciousness.

Principles of Esoteric Healing

We mention these points because they are resumed, in a more coherent fashion, in the later communications of the Master of Medicine, but this apparently is all we hear from this source for another six years. During this time Dion Fortune developed some other inner contacts of a high and unusual quality who, in one way and another, helped and guided her in her esoteric work for the rest of her life. This period included the reception of two book length manuscripts, one being *The Cosmic Doctrine* and the other the gist of *The Esoteric Philosophy of Love and Marriage*.

One of her more active contacts, a very likeable character named Carstairs who claimed to have been an army officer killed on the Ypres salient in the recent war, acted as a general introductor to most of the others, being in effect what in Spiritualist circles would be called a "guide" or "control".

It was this character who came through with an announcement at the beginning of August 1927: "You are about to meet a teacher whom I believe has spoken to you once before, but who will come to you more frequently in the future."

Without further ado this other contact came in, and announced that he would address them on the occult side of physiology, pathology and therapeutics of mind and body, and that this knowledge, although transcending the orthodox canon, would find its place in the structure of rational science.

Accordingly, on 9th August 1927, another book began to be dictated. Its title was *The Principles of Esoteric Medicine*, and by the end of the month three chapters were complete.

The dictated work was interspersed with sessions of question and answer between Dr. Evans and the communicator, about whose identity there was naturally a considerable amount of speculation.

Dion Fortune and the Master of Medicine

The great Renaissance occultist physician Paracelsus (1493-1541)was a popular supposition, but Carstairs intervened in his inimitable style, and advised caution on any public claims as to identity. It was he who suggested using the title "the Master of Medicine".

Being Carstairs, he could not resist putting in a few supplementary hints of his own and eventually identified the last incarnation, through which communication was being channelled, as Dr. Ignez Semmelwiess (1818-65). He was an Austro-Hungarian pioneer of methods of asepsis, before Lister and Pasteur, with the aid of newly invented high resolution microsopes, had identified microbes and bacteria as causes of disease. In maternity wards Semmelweis showed how puerpural or childbed fever, which killed a large percentage of hospitalised patients, could be virtually wiped out if doctors washed their hands in chlorine solution after coming from the morgue.

In response to some direct questions about his identity, the Master of Medicine declined at first to be specific, saying: "I do not see that you need very greatly concern yourselves who I was or what I was. It is sufficient for you that I am willing to teach, and know what I am talking about."

However he later afforded some statements which support Carstairs' identification: "You will never see again what I have seen, when from one ward we were losing eighty percent of normal confinements. We had to close the wards, it was all we could do. I have seen hospitals pulled down because the mortality was such they dare not continue them. They were known as 'Pest-hausen' in my time. They were well named. (This is a double play on words — he refers to the Maternity Clinic at Pest, a town which is now part of Budapest.)

Meetings between the Master of Medicine and Dr. Evans are recorded throughout the next five years, although not as

Principles of Esoteric Healing

frequently as one would have thought, given the initial ambitious intentions. These included writing a book, founding a school and indeed a clinic with special facilities to provide an approach to esoteric medicine on four levels — spiritual, mental, magical and physical.

That is to say it would be a centre manned by medically qualified staff who were also trained in forms of esoteric diagnosis by intuitive and clairvoyant techniques, and who in addition to physical and psychotherapeutic orthodoxies, could provide a magical temple devoted to healing, together with the necessary skills in performing exorcisms and breaking rapports, and the investigation of traumas in past lives. In short, something very much like the establishment fictionally described in *The Secrets of Dr. Taverner*. No small ambition.

The problem seems to have been that with the expansion of Dion Fortune's work and the founding of her Society as a teaching school along general occult lines the more specialised medical line tended to be squeezed out. No doubt, as a practising and very successful medical man, Dr. Evans' time was not entirely his own, to say nothing of his interests in food science research and manufacturing. By 1938 their lives had drifted apart and with it the systematic work with the Master of Medicine.

In 1942 Dion Fortune tried to revive it by seeking other doctors to sit in on the séances, the reason being, which seemed proven by results, that the quality and nature of trance communication depends as much upon the subconscious content of the sitters' minds as upon that of the entranced medium. This applies especially when technical matters or specialities are being discussed. At one point in these latter sessions, (where, interestingly, we still find Maiya Tranchell-Hayes present), the communicator makes this very point:

Dion Fortune and the Master of Medicine

"You understand, do you not, that I am picking up the data from your mind and interpreting from my viewpoint? As I say, I am not a doctor (*sic*) and you are, and I deal with abstract ideas, and I can, as it were, read these from your mind and make use of them in talking to you. If I were discussing with a layman I should not have them to make use of. That is why I have to teach esoteric medicine to one who can supply me with the raw materials. But I deal with abstractions on my plane of consciousness, and you deal with dense matter on your plane of consciousness, and we meet halfway; and I link up my concepts with yours and so make what is abstract, concrete, so that you can make the application."

It is noticeable how, in the presence of a sympathetic medical man, quite detailed clinical discussion could take place. Whereas in the presence of one who, although medically qualified, was sceptical and suspicious and seeking to test the communicator with questions, such as "How would you treat a burn?", the meetings turn out to be abortive and capable only of pursuing generalities.

The attempt to revive this line of work was evidently soon abandoned owing to practical difficulties, not helped by the circumstances of life in wartime Britain. Dion Fortune nonetheless, on a confidential basis, circulated papers entitled "Esoteric Therapeutics" to interested and qualified parties. After the war, and after her death, a more comprehensive version was put together under the title *Esoteric Medicine,* although it was never published. It is this version, counterchecked against the earlier text and original transcripts, that provides the basis for the current work.

Some material has had to be deleted on the grounds that it refers to medical belief and practice that is simply outdated. Much of the text, after all, originates from seventy years ago, as the very names for some of the ailments indicate: infantile paralysis, dementia praecox, and the like. It would also serve

Principles of Esoteric Healing

no purpose to reproduce passing details of clinical cases of yesteryear as remarked upon from time to time.

What has been preserved, and it accounts for about 80% of the material received, are the general principles of esoteric healing. It is hoped that this will prove of interest and of use to alternative therapists and even to members of the medical profession who are interested in another perspective to their craft, whether or not they wish to add intuitive or clairvoyant techniques to their diagnostic skills. It is not inconceivable that some may be unconsciously using their intuitive and psychic abilities more than they think in the course of their treatment of patients. This text will provide hints on how to make such a process less random and unconscious, and buttressed with a reasonably logical metaphysical structure.

Apart from any specialist use, healing in the wider sense applies to any forms of disharmony in the world at large, and therefore can be applied far and wide outside of a narrow clinical context — in work upon oneself as well as upon others.

I have certainly, after a lifetime spent studying occultism in theory and practice, learned much of wide and general application within these pages, which form an excellent and very practical primer of occultism apart from their more specific physical therapeutic intentions.

It will be seen that a certain knowledge of the Tree of Life of the Qabalah is assumed, particularly in the sections that deal with the Etheric Centres, and any reader requiring further guidance along these lines is referred to Dion Fortune's classic work *The Mystical Qabalah*. Those who are already familiar with this system will be interested to note the particular importance given to the crossing of the lateral Paths with those of the vertical Paths. It may be wondered why the topmost crossing point of the 13th and the 14th Paths is not allocated an Etheric Centre but this is in keeping with the

14

Dion Fortune and the Master of Medicine

view that the three Supernal Sephiroth partake very much of a unity because of their spiritual elevation, and if an etheric counterpart should be desired then it may be regarded as part of the complex of the head centres.

It should be said as a point of accuracy that some elements within this work may have come through the mediumship of Margaret Lumley Brown who largely took over Dion Fortune's role in this respect in the Fraternity of the Inner Light after the latter's death in 1946. In the state of the typescript as it has survived it has not been possible to sort out precisely how much she may have contributed. Probably the Asclepios-Apollo temple sequence came through her and possibly some of the material on the Centres. However, she worked very much in the spirit of concluding any unfinished business left by her illustrious predecessor and the work may be considered all of a piece.

Something of her own contribution to occultism can best be appreciated by reference to *Pythoness*, which is to be published as a companion to the present volume.

Gareth Knight

Principles of Esoteric Healing

1.
THE ESOTERIC PHILOSOPHY OF THE ART OF HEALING

The Method of Approach

The physical scientist has his instruments of precision. The esoteric philosopher's instrument is his mind. Physical science proceeds from observation to generalisation, its goal being the discernment of underlying principles. The esoteric philosopher's method is otherwise. He must perforce posit certain fundamentals; without these he has no ground to stand upon.

How shall he obtain his ground of certain conviction, not being based upon observation? He arrives at it by the use of the higher faculties, even if he be not aware of the method he employs. He knows, by becoming that which he seeks to know. This is the only method of true knowledge.

He becomes that which he wishes to know by exalting and intensifying consciously in himself that aspect of himself that corresponds in his nature to the object of his research. This is the way by which meditation yields understanding.

The esoteric philosopher discerns abstractions. The physical scientist is concerned with concretions. The scientifically minded esoteric philosopher and the esoterically aware scientist alone are capable of penetrating the arcana of nature. Every science finds its crown in esoteric philosophy, and esoteric philosophy is the only true teacher of science.

Within these pages we propose to give you the philosophy of the art of healing. It is your task to correlate it with the science of the physical form of man.

Principles of Esoteric Healing

To approach the study of medicine from the esoteric aspect, the mental attitude must be re-orientated. Minds which are accustomed to observe results and penetrate no deeper than immediate causes must disabuse themselves of their limitations by contemplation of the Cosmos as a Unity, and realise that the individual patient is an integral part of that Unity and acts and reacts with the Cosmos as a whole, so that the Earth itself is sick with the sickness of the man.

The study of esoteric medicine is a study of causes — not of effects. A single cause may have diverse effects, according to individual idiosyncracies of reaction. The same disease does not always proceed from the same cause. In the study of medicine from the esoteric standpoint, strive to disabuse your mind from the bondage of the observation of effects, and learn to trace the pathway of transmutation by means of which the disordered forces have come down the planes.

Follow this trail back up the planes until realisation reaches the point where divagation took place. Then, in meditation, return down the planes by the true line of manifestation. Compare the two tracks, plane by plane. Observe what caused the divagation to take place, and seek there the causal remedy. Make there the fundamental adjustments, and then upon each plane make the relative adjustment that shall eliminate the effects of the primary cause which, in turn, have become secondary causes.

There are two errors which are made in systems of medicine.

First, the neglect to ascertain the primary cause of disharmony. This error reduces medical treatment to a sporadic counteracting of effects, leaving the cause untouched. This is the bane of the orthodox.

Second, the attempt to reach the fundamental cause and to deal with it on its own plane, while neglecting to deal with

Esoteric Philosophy of the Art of Healing

those effects which have, in their turn, become secondary causes. This is the bane of the unorthodox.

The battle between the orthodox and the unorthodox is as ancient as the quest for truth. Where shall we find true science? It is to be sought neither in orthodox theory nor in unorthodox practice, but in method. Science does not consist of knowledge, but of method.

The scientific man is the disciplined man. The unscientific man is the undisciplined man. The former has his limitations but is to be relied upon so far as he can go. The latter has his inspirations but is not to be relied upon in all the ways that he goes. The quarrel should therefore shift its basis. It should not be between the orthodox and the unorthodox, but between the scientific method and the unscientific method.

The scientific man, however, should realise that there are other methods of approach besides that of empirical science, and that these methods can yield results. But the unscientific man must also realise that the discoveries which good fortune or intuition may have enabled him to make, cannot be rendered available by any other means than the application of the scientific method.

The scientist must assimilate the pabulum of the esoteric philosopher. The orthodox schools of science are limited by their conservatism. The unorthodox schools are rendered insecure by their lack of foundation in conservative tradition. A quack is a scientific parvenu. He lacks tradition and the stability that it alone can give.

The orthodox schools have deliberately limited themselves to the consideration of matter, and seek to reduce the explanation of vital functions to terms of matter. In this they are sound as far as they go, and such reduction is the true test of theory. That which is expressed on the plane of matter must be capable of expression in terms of matter.

Principles of Esoteric Healing

But where life enters into the process, the final explanation cannot be in terms of matter, for life is not of the plane of matter. When life (the force), functions through matter (the machine), the explanation of the machinery is in terms of matter; but the explanation of life must be in terms of life.

The orthodox schools of science have ever made the mistake of explaining function in terms of machinery. The unorthodox schools have made the mistake of neglecting study of the machinery through which life functions.

The orthodox schools understand well enough the machinery of man. The unorthodox schools guess truly at one and another aspect of the life force in its subtler functions. It is the task of the esoteric healer to synthesise the aspects, contribute a deeper explanation, and thereby reveal the fundamental Unity.

The Spiritual Principles of Healing

Healing is the bringing of the warring and disharmonious factors into equilibrium so that the forces of the Spirit in man can flow down unimpeded. The principles are the same, whether considering a patient who is what you would call physically ill, or when considering anyone who in terms of general life is not in a state of harmonious equilibrium.

All evolutionary progress in the soul of man is healing. So you should not hold too narrow a view of those who may be in need of help in this process. Nor do you need to "inject" forces of the Spirit into your patient. Your aim is to help clear the blocked or twisted channels which impede the flow from his own Spiritual nature.

There is a saying: "Physician, heal thyself!" Unless you yourself be whole, how can you help others to obtain wholeness, integration and harmonisation? Spiritual healing comes

Esoteric Philosophy of the Art of Healing

through the Higher Self. To perform Spiritual healing you must yourself be in contact with your Higher Self, or else how can you operate from that level?

The emotional plane can be manipulated by forces applied at that level without direct Spiritual contact, because you have a mind and are working from the plane above and manipulating these fluid forces. But for the higher forms of healing none other than the higher contact will be of any avail.

Thus you must set yourself this shining goal, for without it all knowledge and all psychic faculties are of limited avail. In your work remember always the important factor of gaining contact with your Higher Self. If you give this its due, and foremost place in the planning of your time, you will find that all other things will fall into their rightful place.

Put first things first. The Higher Self is always of a healing and harmonious nature. It is the "magical bodies" on the astral or emotional plane which carry imperfections. The Higher Self can be undeveloped, but is perfect as far as its goes. Being composed of the three upper levels of the planes of consciousness, it contains no imperfections in itself.

Always regard your patient as a soul expressing itself through different vehicles of consciousness and not as a piece of machinery that has gone wrong. Remember this even when treating what would appear to be purely physical conditions, such as an accident case. It is true that a man may have suffered an accident to his physical body and therefore needs treatment for that, but even here the causes may lie deeper. He may have been what is called "accident prone" due to a psychological condition, and the task of the Healer Priest should be to bring about harmony between the soul and all its vehicles.

There is a true need for the ministry of healing. It may be true that some people can only learn through physical suffering, yet

Principles of Esoteric Healing

for others evolutionary progress may be hampered by having an inefficient physical vehicle, or they may be denied the opportunity of learning through experience because of a faulty personality instrument.

People are only ready for help in the subtler ways of healing when they ask for it, either consciously or subconsciously — for there are more ways of asking than by direct appeal. Combined with this there must be a genuine desire to co-operate and help as much as possible from their own side. Without these two factors it is unwise and useless to try and help them — further learning is needed through experience of the conditions of which they are in. These conditions may be emotional or mental or the reactions of those levels of consciousness to mundane circumstances.

When considering how to bring about the harmonisation of a person you have first to estimate what they need. This question of diagnosis is the most difficult thing, for unless you can determine the fundamental cause of a disharmony you cannot adequately attempt to treat it, for merely to treat symptoms may aggravate the condition.

What a person needs depends upon their "grade" in terms of spiritual evolution. What a person wants may not be what in fact they need. All the personality is aware of is its symptoms, of the lack of health or opportunity, and not the remote causes which may have occasioned it. Thus they are not in the best position to prescribe for themselves.

It must be recognised that the coming through and strengthening contact of the Higher Self with the personality is no small proceeding and can be a difficult time of stress. It cannot be helped if the personality is affected, whether in the form of "nerves", or some kind of ill health that sets in at the time. In some way or another there is always some outward mark of what takes place inwardly. Inner conflicts — according to their type — weaken the physical vehicle and can set up very strong disturbances within it which, if not checked, may end in definite illness.

Esoteric Philosophy of the Art of Healing

It is very necessary that those who aspire to become Spiritual Healers know as much of the ordinary methods of healing as the average doctor of the present time. You should have a broad basis of established scientific skill and knowledge, particularly from the diagnostic point of view. You must get your feet firmly rooted in the scientific earth, so to speak, before getting your head into the rarified air of psychological speculation. You will not then diagnose an organic disease as a functional one.

Primarily, trained people are required for this work. You must learn the practice of mental magic — this is the special field in the New Age, when, with more widespread knowledge of the Unseen worlds, there will be an increasing number of people who will need healing on mental magical lines.

The Work and Essentials of a true Physician

I would have you grasp as one of your fundamentals that the physician's task is to re-educate his patients as well as to treat them. To teach his patients as well as to treat them. To teach patients how to fight disease mentally. To teach them how to free themselves from inhibitions, and to lay hold consciously upon the sources of vitality.

In this task the work falls into three distinct phases:
1. the treatment of the physical body;
2. the re-education of mind and emotions;
3. the revelation of the possibilities of the Higher Self.

The true doctor is as much priest as physician. The original doctors were always priests and it is through the divorce between theology and medicine that both have fallen away from the wisdom of the ancient world. There is the old story of the blind man who carried on his shoulders the lame man; both arrived safely at their destination. So it is with the science of the soul and the science of the body. The doctor is the blind

Principles of Esoteric Healing

man — he can do, but he cannot see the subtle causes in the soul. The priest is the man with the vision — he knows, but he cannot do.

Our aim is to teach the priests of medicine; and just as a priest has his choristers and his acolytes and his servitors, so must all those who assist in the healing art be trained and dedicated, because the work is done largely in the Unseen, and the mental atmosphere with which you surround your patients is the chief part of the cure. As well might you place a hospital beside a stagnant drain as seek to heal patients in a place of bickering, or of impurity, or of selfishness.

The surgeon trains his sense of touch. The priest of medicine must cultivate and purify his own soul and his own character, for he heals as much by what he _is_ as by what he does. If your own soul is disturbed, if your own life problems are unsolved, if your heart is impure, you are like a surgeon coming to the operating table or the labour ward with unclean hands.

Just as in the old days surgeons infected their patients with their hands and with the objects they contacted in the wards, so in these days, evolution having advanced, and men and women having become more sensitive, doctors and nurses may infect the sick with their minds, and with the mental atmosphere of the places in which they are put. Dedicate your life, purify your character, and exalt your soul if you would be a priest of medicine.

There are two things you must give your patients — interest and beauty — to nourish the soul as well as the body. We seek to teach the significance of the mental and emotional factors in medicine, and, to those who can understand and appreciate them, the occult factors that lie beyond.

You will be given certain knowledge concerning the occult side of psychology, pathology and therapeutics of both mind and body. This knowledge, though transcending the orthodox

Esoteric Philosophy of the Art of Healing

canons, will be found to fit in its place in the structure of rational science.

In this line of teaching we do not proceed from observed particulars to a general principle, but from a general principle we depart in quest of particulars. In the school of esoteric medicine we are trained to start all our research work with meditation upon cosmic principles applicable to the matter, and from one single general principle bring the mind down the planes, watching the applications unfold themselves to consciousness at each level.

The results so obtained must then be submitted to counterchecking by the methods taught by inductive science. If true, they will pass that test and take their place within the canon of scienctific knowledge.

It is the life forces themselves with which we work in esoteric medicine. It is those life forces as effected on the astral plane, and affecting the physical plane through the etheric sub-planes, that we study and work with, and we control that from the higher planes. That is the essence of occult therapeutics.

The work is done on the astral. The results are obtained in the subtle ethers. The manifestation shows forth in mind and in body. It is a method of great subtlety, and the instruments of its operations are those of the trained faculties.

The Scope of Esoteric Medicine

In teaching esoteric medicine generally, we may either continue from the point where orthodox medicine stops, or bring through entirely fresh concepts of a revolutionary nature, based on esoteric principles of which the orthodox are ignorant. Two subjects especially engage our attention, however, because they are so inadequately dealt with by medical science.

One is endocrinology from the point of view of how emotional and mental conditions affect the endocrines, and so, by regulating these, a method of regulating the endocrines may be

Principles of Esoteric Healing

obtained. Much advance has been made in medicine from the physical end on this subject, namely the effect of the endocrines on the personality, and the alteration of endocrine action by chemical means.

The other subject is the treatment of the insane, as present treatment is such a hit and miss method, without really understanding why certain treatments sometimes produce certain results.

I am not only concerned with mental and psychological healing. I am concerned primarily with consciousness and all that affects it. The endocrine balance, emotional and astral states, complexes and psychological difficulties on the mental level, and on the plane above, the influence of past lives acting through the "magical bodies" — the sum total being represented by what we call the "ghost" — all affect consciousness.

I am concerned primarily with the vital processes of life itself, and only secondarily with the machinery through which it manifests; orthodox medicine thinks only of the machinery and neglects consciousness itself.

This comprises the esoteric anatomy and physiology of the subtle bodies of man, including the functions, pathologies and treatment of the Seven Centres in the "Four Worlds". The influence of the Centres on the endocrine glands and their treatment — which includes psychology because mental states upset the Centres. Esoteric diagnosis including the use of the Brow Centre and auric readings. The occult pathologies including Rapports and their treatment. Also the constitution and work of a Healing Temple, with particular reference to the training of its priesthood. The formulation of the god forms in therapeutic work and their practical applications.

In the course of all this we shall be covering a vast field. Many points may be touched in passing without giving a full explanation. I am covering the ground in broad sweeps in order that you may have a framework, and it is up to you to work over that framework, filling in the details through personal realisation and experience.

2.
ESOTERIC ANATOMY

The Development of the Subtle Bodies in the Light of Evolution

Anatomy can only be understood in the light of evolution. We will therefore consider the stages of the development of the vehicles of man, commencing with the nucleus of a Divine Spark of Pure Spirit whose reactions are stereotyped according to the conditions of the 7th Cosmic Plane.

We observe the acquirement of a further set of stereotyped reactions. These are known as the spiritual qualities, and constitute a 6th Plane body.

From the interplay of these, acting on themselves, are developed abstract ideas. These abstract ideas constitute the 5th Plane vehicle of consciousness.

It will be observed that the three higher vehicles are self-determined upon a Cosmic basis and are not influenced by their environment. This is an important point, for it means that the Individuality or Higher Self is stable and constant, and being governed exclusively by Cosmic Law, is harmonious and is not liable to disease. It can therefore be taken as a constant or norm in all therapeutic calculations.

Let us conceive then of this three-fold Individuality evolving throughout eternity. It has for its keynote the Ray type to which it belongs, but in the course of its evolution it passes through the sub-Ray phases. Conceive this abstract Entity conducting its evolution by building up for itself bodies of ideas, of feelings and of sensations, and from the experiences

Principles of Esoteric Healing

thus derived, abstracting the essence and using it for its growth.

In considering the anatomy of the complete human being, you will perceive that you have upon one hand a purely abstract, three-fold consciousness which is immortal and harmonious, which is, indeed, made in the Image and Likeness of God. On the other hand you have a four-fold organisation which is in the image and likeness of the Solar System. The analogies of the Individuality must be sought in the Cosmos, and of the Personality in the Solar System.

The Individuality represents the sun in the universe of the Personality; but while the Individuality is immortal, eternal, harmonious and formless, the Personality is mortal, being resolved into its component parts at the conclusion of each incarnation, and ceasing to be. It is inharmonious, being a world of warring forces ruled in varying degree by higher consciousness.

What then is the nexus between these two divergent forms of existence? The Individuality, it is true, extracts the essence of each Personality it builds, but this essence is purely abstract and contains no element of form, and no element of concrete memory. Does, therefore, any form of concrete existence carry over from the past? It does, and it is known as the "Ghost".

The Doctrine of the Ghost

Thus far we have considered matters well known to all students of esoteric science. We will now consider matters not so well known, and I will proceed to teach you what we call the "Doctrine of the Ghost". This is an extraordinarily important point in esoteric pathology and therapeutics.

I would have you note that the Ghost is not the same thing as the Fate. The Fate is the abstract essence of the past, acting as causation in the present and the future.

28

Esoteric Anatomy

The Ghost is a distinct organisation, and it will be best understood by reminding you of the doctrine of thought-forms. Every concrete image clearly formulated in the imagination becomes a thought-form, and is capable of independent existence for a greater or lesser period. The Ghost is the thought-form of self-consciousness plus memory, or in other words, the Ego-complex. This remains attached by a tenuous thread of association to the Individuality.

The popular esoteric doctrine of Seed Atoms is based on an imperfect appreciation of this phenomenon. This Ego-complex determines the form into which the bodies of the Personality are cast in the next incarnation, and the Fate determines the manner in which the forces play through them.

The Ghost, therefore, is a composite picture of all the forms and all the memories of all past incarnations, and it may best be compared to the series of reflections in a pair of mirrors.

The Ghost itself is never more than one incarnation old, but it holds in its memory an image of the previous Ghost, and is affected thereby; and that Ghost has in its memory an image of the Ghost before itself, and so on down the series. It is these Ghosts that are evoked when the images of past incarnations are awakened.

Disease is the checking and thwarting of life; and certain forms of disease are carried over by the Ghost. You will get a good deal of explanation of congenital malformations in this conception of the Ghost, because the malformation may be due to malformation in the Ghost which is due to deflections of the life force in the past.

If a person has a thwarted life and suffers from repression of one of the three great instincts, the Ghost will be malformed and certain types of malformation may be present at birth if the thwarting is more than one incarnation old. Or if the thwarting took place in the last life, it may recur as organic disease at the age at which the thwarting took place previously. There

Principles of Esoteric Healing

are methods of dealing with this therapeutically. It is achieved by keeping open, despite the Fate, channels which were previously blocked.

I would advise you to collect cases and collate the specific instances of the application of this theory concerning the Ghost. I may tell you that such irregularities of form are due to malformations of the etheric double and go back many incarnations. You will not cure these in a single incarnation, but you can prevent their recurrence by breaking up the thought-form which caused them.

Have you noticed a tendency to cruelty in any case of chronic physical abnormality? If this tendency is a key note in the character it may be the case of an exalted ego striving for expression — a thwarted autocrat. In such a case try to work the autocratic character out and purify it. The defect will not be cured physically, but its effect on the life may be very materially reduced.

Do not forget to distinguish between mechanical injuries to the foetus, either *in utero* or during delivery, from true malformations of the etheric double. Confusion is sometimes made between the two. One is purely mechanical and does not affect consciousness; the other is deep rooted in the past. One who is crippled as the result of injury, even if the injury takes place at birth, will not show the same defects of temperament as one in whom the cause is congenital. The mentality is quite different.

The subtle bodies evolve, as far as the lower four are concerned, as the result of experiences undergone in incarnation. The upper three are the production of Cosmic evolution and do not change their form, but unfold their possibilities as the result of absorbing the essence of incarnation.

Note carefully, however, that they only absorb that which is harmonised and brought under Cosmic Law. All the

Esoteric Anatomy

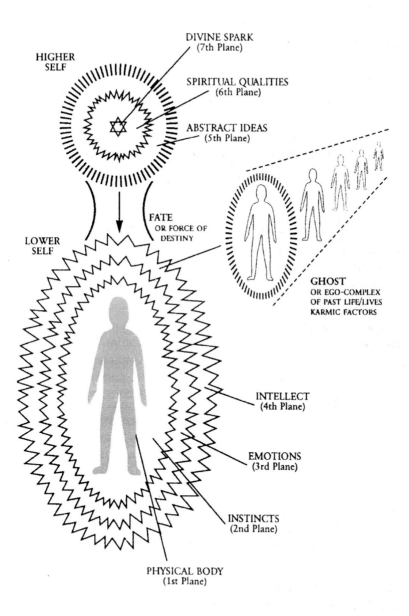

The Subtle Bodies, the Ghost and the Fate

Principles of Esoteric Healing

unharmonised residuum is absorbed by the Ghost. This is a very important point, for the Individuality is a great reservoir of health and harmony. So called spiritual healing is accomplished by bringing the powers of the Individuality to bear on the powers of the Personality. The mechanism is the same as that of initiation.

It is to the Ghost we must look for predestined disease. The Ghost is not a living entity, but a thought-form, and the methods of dispelling thought-forms are applicable to it, and if successfully applied on the astral plane, or plane of memory images, will effectually cut at the roots of the disease, and render it amenable to physical therapeutic methods.

Therein you have the distinction between mental healing and physiological medicine, and esoteric healing as I teach it.

Physiological medicine treats symptoms, but does not touch causes. Spiritual healing touches primary causes but leaves effects, which in their turn leave causes undealt with. Esoteric medicine combines the two.

Spiritual healing brings the Individuality through into control of the Personality vehicles, as in initiation. Mental healing deals with the thought forms of the patient, whether these be extruded and overshadowing, as in the Ghost, or dissociated in the subconscious mind. And note this: the subconscious mind is a Ghost in the making. The subconscious mind in this incarnation is the Ghost in the next incarnation.

The Relationship of the Subtle Bodies to Astrology

It is not necessary here to go into the details of the evolution, or more strictly speaking, the development of the subtle bodies on the involutionary arc. Suffice to say that such bodies are mere aggregations of reaction potentialities which are organised according to the type of the corresponding planet.

Each plane corresponds to a planet, the reason being that that planet was evolved in the course of the evolution of that

Esoteric Anatomy

plane. You will see, therefore, that the real essence of that planet is the same as the real essence of that plane, and as the subtle body which corresponds to that plane is evolved under the conditions of the plane, it is obvious that it will be typical of that plane. The planet is the grand type of that plane, and therefore the unevolved subtle body will be like a miniature planet.

I will now give you an important astrological hint. It is not so much that the planets affect the corresponding bodies, as that planet and bodies are affected by the same conditions, and react to them in the same way. Therefore the esoteric physician, although he rightly concerns himself with correspondences, does not unduly concern himself with the times and seasons of the astrologer.

For though astrology is a true science of correspondences, its popular presentations are full of superstition. People take up occultism because they like the spectacular. It is an intellectual gambling instinct to which it appeals; but occult science is just as careful, just as accurate, just as slow and just as limited and limiting as any other science.

The mistake the astrologer makes is the failure to recognise the fact that the influences of a planet remain on the plane of that planet, or more accurately speaking, the influences to which plane the planet and body react, and of which the planet can be used as indicator, operate only on that plane, and only affect physical conditions by being translated down the planes through the vehicles, and up the planes conversely.

That is to say, should the influence of Mercury affect the mental body, or an influence of Venus the upper astral, or of Mars the lower astral, then those influences operate on the specific plane. Mercury would affect the mind, or rather mind would react to the mental condition of the plane. But conditions on the material plane would not be affected except insofar as the subject allowed them to be affected.

Principles of Esoteric Healing

For instance, if mental disturbances upset his mental balance, rash judgements might cause him to act foolishly on the physical plane and so disturb mundane conditions. That is an important practical point.

Astrology, therefore, is useful in determining the native constitution of the subject, but is all too apt to act through suggestion when used for prognosis. Nativities are useful, but progressions are of dubious value at the best of times, and frequently do more harm than good, because of the power of suggestion and the fact that the intuitive astrologer cannot but be influenced by the hopes and fears of the querant, and returns an answer in accordance with the preconceived ideas rather than with the facts of the case.

It is quite impossible for any astologer to say what modifications experience of life has brought in character and reaction capacity. Therefore my counsel is that a nativity is useful, but a progression is both useless and harmful.

The Relationship between Man and the Universe

You must remember firstly that all things are tidal — flux and reflux. The universe is ruled and determined by a series of rhythms and the rhythms do not synchronise. Their modes are different and they lace in and out of each other. One will be flowing, another ebbing, and a third changing from ebb to flow, and a fourth from flow to ebb. And those which are ebbing assist each other, and those which are flowing assist each other, and ebb opposes flow.

All these rhythms have their bearing upon the planets, and the things of the mundane world may be assigned to one or another according to the doctrine of signatures. And the parts of man respond to these different rhythms. There is a rhythm of Mars, a rhythm of Jupiter, a rhythm of Venus. An old planet like Saturn has a slow cold rhythm. A new planet like the

Esoteric Anatomy

Moon, a rapid alternation. Venus and Mars are capricious in their changes.

Each of these correspond to a phase of creation, and in these phases of creation different aspects of mankind were built up. There was a phase of creation in which the bony structure was developed, a phase in which the blood channels were developed, and if you examine this you will find that these phases of development correspond to the epochs wherein creation may be conceived as taking place on a planetary sphere. But these spheres are not the planets as we know them, for these are but the shrunken remains of the spheres which were evolved in the Solar System.

Remember, the different systems of a living being have their correspondences with the planets, and knowing the planetary tides you will know how the phases work in these systems. There will be a phase when all that concerns the circulation of the blood is being opposed to that which concerns the bony structure; their planets are in opposition and diseases in which the blood stream is concerned will meet with opposition.

Some understanding of these tides is essential to the wise physician. A sound knowledge of the science of astrology, not in the usual vulgar use of it for fortune telling, but as revealing the relationship between mind and matter, and the reaction to the tides.

The question of vital resistance cannot be considered only in relation to emotions but to Cosmic influences as well. A tender emotion arises with the rise of Venus; a war-like emotion with the rise of Mars. These matters must not be overlooked. Learn the relationship between the parts of the microcosm and the parts of the macrocosm, and study the rhythms of the macrocosm and you will know much about the rhythms of the microcosm.

Seek always to build — to build upon the positive side. Never instruct your patients to overcome a vice or weakness; inspire them to develop the quality which compensates it. Never

Principles of Esoteric Healing

suffer yourself or others to dwell upon negative images. Dwell upon the positive — the constructive — that you may build up. For when you dwell upon the negative, you destroy.

You will never inspire a man or woman to do better by holding up an image of their own evil. Hold up the image of their possible achievement and they will follow it. If you hold up an image of weakness you do but reinforce those weaknesses in their own souls.

All substances possess a subtle aspect as well as a dense, and the subtle nature of man will respond more readily to the subtle aspect of substance. Use the alterative purpose. To all metallic or crystalline drugs there is an electrical aspect. To all vegetable drugs there is an etheric aspect. The effect of a drug is different when it is desiccated to when it is fresh. There are potencies which are not revealed by analysis.

The best medicaments are made from herbs freshly gathered and infused and these herbs should be gathered with consideration for the phases of the moon and planets to which they correspond, because the subtle aspect is affected by them. There are plants belonging to Luna which, when gathered on the waning moon are inert in their subtle aspect; whereas if gathered on the full moon are highly potent.

You must also distinguish between the patient in whom the subtle bodies are dominant and the patient in whom the dense body is dominant.

The Fourfold Constitution of Man
The Four Elements and Types

In our Western Tradition we usually give the fourfold classification of Man. There are four types, each of which can be subdivided into denser and subtler aspects.

1. the Physical or Phlegmatic;
2. the Emotional, Watery or Bilious;

Esoteric Anatomy

3. the Mental or Airy;

4. the Spiritual or Fiery.

These four reduce to two types, with a higher and lower aspect to each, and these two types may be characterised as Extrovert or Introvert.

The *lower* aspect of the *Extrovert* is the *Physical* type, who lives in sensation.

The *higher* aspect of the *Extrovert* is the *Mental* type who lives in his cogitations upon his sensations.

Both these types are positive on the physical plane.

The *lower* aspect of the *Introvert* is the *Emotional* type, who lives in his emotions; that is to say, in how he feels about his sensations.

The *higher* aspect of the *Introvert* is the *Spiritual* type, who is also turned into the consideration of subjective reactions, but he is considering his reactions in relation to the Cosmos and to evolution. He is considering himself as part of a whole, and his relations fundamentally are to the Cosmos, not to the world of appearances.

In actual practice you will distinguish the types by observing the predominant quality in their make-up.

The Treatment of the Four Types

In dealing with patients you should take into consideration the proportion of the elements in the constitution. This was sound practice in the old medicine. They divided them into four divisions, each corresponding to one of the four Elements, and your therapy should take this into account.

When dealing with the Phlegmatic type their prescriptions would be of the earth — earthy. That is to say predominantly mineral drugs.

Principles of Esoteric Healing

When dealing with the Water or Bilious temperament they would tend to prescribe vegetable drugs and herbs.

In this respect, note that there is a difference of quality in a substance of vegetable origin which has been reduced to the level of an inorganic salt. Therefore, when using vegetable remedies, follow the lore of the old herbalists and employ, not vegetable essences, but the vegetable teas and distillations.

Then in dealing with the Airy or Mental temperament they would give animal remedies, with properties of animal substance; the mind and the endocrines are in intimate association.

In dealing with the Fiery, Spiritual temperament they would use the mind only; it is all it requires.

But in all of this you must distinguish in theory and combine in practice. Only the idiot is all body. Only the feeble minded is purely body and emotions. Only the rare saints are all spirit. Use the four-fold remedies for the four-fold man. Give him something of each but adjust the proportion to the proportion of the Elements in his nature.

This is a very practical point. Do you see its significance? It is a system of correspondences. But remember it is always a question of proportion. All four aspects must be touched.

When dealing with a patient, the root of whose problem may be upon the mental level, look beyond the physical manifestation, because it may well be that a large proportion of that individual's consciousness is prevented from expression owing to the physical conditions, but nevertheless is present in the soul. Therefore you would treat that individual as being, shall we say, an Airy type, if the mentality were developed but not being expressed. You must treat, that is to say, what he really is and not what he appears to be. For that diagnosis, clairvoyant powers may be necessary, and you should endeavour to develop them.

Esoteric Anatomy

With regard to the four temperaments, the Physical is well enough understood by medical science and you need little instruction upon that. The Mental is increasingly being studied and understood by the psychologist. The Spiritual temperament is so rare as to be negligible. It is the Astral temperament which is the problem, and is not understood by either physiologist or psychologist.

You must remember that the physical body has its subtle counterpart in the etheric body, and many forms of treatment act on that. Light treatment and electrical treatment act on the etheric body, and so do colloidal substances and high homeopathic potencies. In all of these things you are getting off the plane of dense matter.

In a sense there is a physician appropriate to each type of patient. For the physical body — the doctor or surgeon. For the mind — the psychologist. For the spirit — the priest. What of the astral body? Who ministers to that?

When the dealing with a physical or mental case, doctor or psychologist may be adequate, but when they come to deal with a case which is neither physical nor mental, they are not. They are likely to say to the patient "you are not ill." Nevertheless, the patient is suffering, and his working capacity is impaired or destroyed. If you were that person you would think that you were ill. Treat the suffering not the physical conditions. Yet the mind of that person is not so sick that he can be certified. It is his emotions that are ailing. It is an astral case — a Watery type.

Who ministers to the astral body — the Watery temperament — when it falls sick? Very often the quack! But there he may be a true healer, and capable of curing cases which neither the doctor nor the psychologist can touch. When you come to deal with the Watery temperament you could well use the methods of the quack, and I do not say that invidiously. I mean that if you investigate the various quack systems you will find that each one that is able to show results,

Principles of Esoteric Healing

and is not purely purse snatching, is based on a natural law of the astral plane, and you will find that they will repay investigation.

Take the different systems that compete with orthodox medicine. If you look at them in bulk you may well consider them as trash. But take that trash and distil its essence and you may well find a truth. For no one can build a system which is altogether fallacious unless he move on from place to place as did the old fashioned pill vendor at the country fair. Find the essence of the system and you may have a treatment for the astral condition.

You will find in breathing systems, moving systems, all sorts and conditions of systems, something worthy of note. And when you approach the Watery temperament you have to approach it through the appropriate "watery" channel. The potent factor in the Watery temperament is the power of the imagination to contact the vitality, due fundamentally to the very close rapport existing between souls of that type and the Earth Spirit of the corresponding level. That is a very important point.

The Airy or Mental temperament has an affiliation with the group mind of the race and of humanity itself. People of that type can be thrown into sickness by any severe calamity to the human race — an earthquake — a volcanic eruption — or a tidal wave — in the remote parts of the world which cause great loss and suffering. It will have its effect upon them. You cannot treat the Mental type unless you take into consideration their relationship to the Spirit of the Earth.

3.
THE CLASSIFICATION OF DISEASES

Harmony is the law of the universe. Were it not so, long before this the solar system would have been destroyed by friction. Divagations from harmony have primarily a Cosmic origin. Were there no disharmony in the macrocosm there could be none in the microcosm. Disharmony originates with the development of free will, and is representative of a transition phase.

In the initial stages of an evolution, when all is governed by pre-established conditions already harmonised, all is harmony. In the final stages of an evolution, when self-consciousness has caused free will to become approximated to God's Will, or Cosmic Law, all is harmony. But in the intervening stage there is disharmony while the lessons of experience are being acquired and adjustments are being made.

In the Cosmos, however, conscious compensating forces are ever at work. Equally therefore, compensating forces must be available for the microcosm, which is man. On this principle is based the science of esoteric medicine.

In the diagnosis of the individual case, seek the point where the microcosm has departed from the law of the macrocosm, and then seek in your tentative healing arts to ally yourself with the corresponding compensating forces whose task it would be to remedy a similar divagation in the Cosmos. And remember that these forces are conscious, are intelligent, and are in fact of the plane of life, though their lives are not as your life.

Use life forces on the planes of life. That is correct practice. But it is incorrect practice to use life forces save through the

Principles of Esoteric Healing

machinery appropriate to the plane upon which their corrective influence is desired. For example, you cannot use mind on matter, but must perforce find a vehicle of manifestation. Mind acts on the ethers only, not on matter. When it is desired to act direct upon matter, the form of manifestation of the requisite aspect of life must be found. Hence the doctrine of signatures.

The Types of Disease

There are many different types of disease. Learn to discern the types first and discern them in terms of origin. See when the body is poisoning the mind; when the mind is poisoning itself; when the mind is being poisoned on the plane of mind; and when the mind is being starved on the plane of spirit.

Classify in terms of causation, not in terms of the plane on which symptoms appear. You would not classify a fever as a disease of the forehead, of the chest, or of the stomach because the rash appears first on the skin of that place.

Some of the types of disease are of physical origin, some spiritual, some of the plane of the mind. Some are objective, some are subjective, but you will never have subjective mental disease that does not speedily acquire an objective aspect, for whatever the mind disturbance may be, it is not limited to the subjective.

The Principles of Physical Disease

We will now consider briefly the principles of physical disease. These diseases may be primarily physical, or secondarily physical. That is to say, they may originate from causes in the physical body or from causes in the subtle bodies; but as long as you have a physical result, physical methods of treatment are indicated.

The Classification of Diseases

Supposing, for instance, an abnormal astral condition produces a toxic condition of the blood. You cannot cure that toxic condition, the disease in the physical body, until you have adjusted the astral. However much you neutralise the poisons, more will be formed.

But after you have removed the astral condition, a considerable period may elapse before nature, unassisted, will eliminate the poisons from the system. And as long as the poisons remain in the system they will tend to reproduce the emotional state which gave rise to them.

Therefore, never be content to counteract symptoms without seeking their cause. But until the symptoms have ceased to manifest upon the physical plane, counteract them energetically on that plane. Do you apprehend the significance of this? Deal with the two conditions simultaneously.

For instance, many cases of chronic constipation will yield to mental treatment. But until the mental treatment has taken effect you must employ laxatives. Gradually reduce the drug element as the mental element becomes effective.

Diseases which manifest in the physical body may be divided into two main divisions — etheric disease and physical disease.

Etheric disease is so named because faulty function is apparent in the etheric aspect of the physical body, thus producing faulty functioning and changes of condition. Note that it is only when the etheric mould itself is affected that organic changes take place, and organic changes indicate that you should look beyond the etheric body for causes.

Physical diseases are caused by interference with the function of the physical machine. These can be entirely and adequately explained in terms of matter.

Principles of Esoteric Healing

It will be seen, however, from the foregoing explanation that in actual practice all diseases will end by interfering with the functioning of the physical machine, and therefore can be reduced to an explanation in terms of matter. When, however, the functioning of the physical vehicle becomes faulty, the corresponding function of the etheric counterpart is inhibited, and so the ethers are also affected.

Always bear in mind the fact that man is a composite mechanism, and in life the functioning of the planes cannot be separated in actual practice, though for a correct apprehension they must be distinguished in theory. The art and skill of medicine has its source in a mental attitude which recognises the distinction in theory and apprehends the interaction in practice.

This, then, is the prime division between
   a) diseases which originate in matter, and
   b) diseases which have their origin in divagations of the life force, which manifest in the etheric body and react on the physical body.

These may be divided again into two broad divisions: mechanical defects, and poisonings. Under the latter head are included deprivations of essentials.

Again, these are interacting, for mechanical abnormalities will give rise to poisonings through faulty functionings; and poisonings will give rise to mechanical irregularities, such as congestion and hypertrophy.

It is necessary in all these matters, if a true understanding is to be arrived at, to maintain the philosophical attitude which discerns the nature of the essence of the disharmony and correctly assigns it to its plane and classification. But it is equally necessary in actual practice to remember that healing is an art as well as a science; and art has been defined as the realisation of proportion.

The Classification of Diseases

We can speak then of:

1. vitality diseases;
2. mechanical diseases;
3. poisonings.

In each case classification will depend not on the nature of the symptoms, but in the nature of their origin. Among mechanical diseases are included all traumas; and among poisonings all bacterial infections. The practical application of this classification can readily be seen by considering actual cases.

Diseases which occur entirely from mechanical or toxic causes on the physical plane, (including infections), are nevertheless to be considered from the standpoint of vitality, for they represent the overcoming of the vitality, whether because the vitality was low or the external pressure was high.

If you have realised the way disease reacts up and down the planes, you will also be able to realise the way in which therapeutic processes react up and down the planes.

Let us take the different forms of insanity. Insanity is usually classified as mental disease, and all those showing predominately mental symptoms are herded together for treatment, or lack of it. But there are vital insanities due to disease of the emotions; mechanical insanities due to injuries to the brain; and toxic insanities.

You would, however, place an insanity due to a tumour of the brain to a vital cause, for all neoplasms come under that heading; they are obsessional throughout the body and the blood. This includes what I choose to call tumours of the blood. I use that term expressly because I wish you to understand the significance of any germ or new growth. Whether it be a foetus or a cancer the mechanism is the same. You will find a great deal of significance in that if you think it out. Think about a foetus — is it not an obsession of the womb?

Principles of Esoteric Healing

If an obsession be the entry of another centre of living consciousness into a vehicle built by a soul, and the utilisation of that vehicle by an alien life, are not such things as bacterial infections also obsessional in nature? There you get the key again.

And if you think out the process of the normal foetus and the medium of inception, you will get a key to the problem of the abnormal foetus — the malignant growth.

There is a certain disease of the blood, well known in tropical countries, in which very large corpuscles in bacterial form, eat their smaller brothers. This is an obsession of the large corpuscles. It is an external life which has come in and it is not, strictly speaking, a bacterial infection but the result of a very decided astral infection. Do you follow?

The process is this: after very severe malarial infection, long continued and with great debilitation, the system is open to invasions of other forms of life, and these come, not physically, but astrally. I give this merely as a passing instance. Such a disease could only be cured by taking the man to a temperate climate where the obsessing entity of that particular sort could not follow. But usually he would be in such a state before the observed invasion takes place that he would not survive the journey. But there is a distinction between malarial infection in the case in which the obsessing entities have a physical form, and the astral invasion in which the incoming entities have no physical form, but build it entirely out of the body of the host. Therefore these should be classified with the tumours, being of obsessional origin, and not with the toxic diseases which have a physical origin.

Diseases of the Etheric Double

We will next consider the diseases of the etheric double. The etheric double is the physical channel of etheric force. It is

The Classification of Diseases

function that builds form, and etheric function lays down fibres and molecules. They build up about the cells, they do not generate the cells. The etheric double is the system of magnetic stresses which is the framework into which each cell of the physical body is built. It is the etheric double, or soul of the cell, which exercises the well known selective power of cell metabolism.

The etheric double it is which responds to electrical treatment and light treatment, for rays are carried by the ethers. Light, whether visible or invisible, is a potent physical therapeutic agent. Very important effects can be obtained by the use of coloured light, but the manner of procurement of colouration of light is important. There is a difference between a blue light and light which is stained blue. It is of little effect to pass white light through a blue glass; it is not blue light it is a stained light.

The best way to obtain a coloured ray is by reflected light. White light reflected from a blue surface will be actively blue. It is possible to obtain an active ray of coloured light if sunlight be concentrated through a crystal — a natural crystal of the colour required. You can thus obtain an active red light by concentrating a beam of sunlight through a ruby.

You can obtain potencies of different forces by a direct beam of light from either the sun or an electric spark through a gem appropriately cut, which is their sacred stone, and that is a thing worth knowing. Remarkable psychic effects can be obtained by transmitting a Mars ray through a ruby, a Venus ray through an emerald, a Moon ray through a moonstone. If the eye is concentrated on a gem in a dark room, the gem being placed in a screen, strange results follow. This is a ready method of coming into touch with the potency desired. This is a method too potent to apply to a patient in most cases, but you can apply it to yourself, and through your own vehicle transmit the force.

Principles of Esoteric Healing

Sound is not a healing agent in itself, but affects the astral body by affecting the emotions through the imagination.

Whenever there is any condition present in any of the four lower vehicles it will produce a corresponding reaction in the others of the four. For instance, a mental exaltation or emotional depression, provided they be acute enough, can be traced clinically by the ordinary methods.

Every insanity has its characteristic metabolism.

The question which has to be decided is whether toxic conditions are the result of an inner disturbance and are producing the reactions in consciousness. Many an abnormal astral or mental condition has its origin in the physical body, just as many an abnormal physical condition has its origin in the subtle bodies. Learn to put your finger on the point where the departure from harmony takes place, and not merely discern the incidence of the symptoms.

The vitamins and all forms of radiation therapy act on the etheric double, and through that on the physical body. The vitamin in a plant or other substance is etheric not physical, and that is why it cannot be isolated. The study of these two aspects is important to you.

Remember that in the highways and byways of therapeutics you may often light upon something worth finding. Many quack methods affect the etheric double, and they are worth investigating. Their function is not in the system but in the application.

Diseases of the etheric double are of two types: those which originate internally and those which originate externally .

The internal origin may be due either to astral conditions at the present time, or the influences of the Ghost. The former are usually acute; the latter chronic.

The Classification of Diseases

The external origin of etheric disease depends on all manner of ruptures, displacements and unco-ordinations between the patient and the etheric aspect of the universe. It is, in fact, a failure of correspondences and the aim should be to put the patient in touch with natural forces. For the etheric double feeds and breathes and excretes on its own plane, exactly as does the physical body on its plane.

Failure to receive the due etheric nutriment of forces causes starvation of the etheric body. Failure to express the etheric forces causes a toxic condition of the etheric body. Etheric forces are drawn from the Earth, from the Sun, from vegetation and, under certain conditions, from other human beings.

The etheric body can be dealt with in two ways — by the etheric forces of the operator or by the etheric forces of nature. To deal with it by the etheric forces of the operator is a method which should be reserved solely for grave emergencies. It is equivalent to a blood transfusion. The best method to employ is the contact of the vital forces through natural sources. On earth, air, sunlight and vegetation, for these are all impersonal.

Diseases of the Astral Plane

We come next to consideration of the diseases of the lower astral. These are all due to repression or deflection of the life force as expressed through the three primary instincts, whether in their lower or their higher forms.

This deflection or repression of force may occur on one or other of the planes of form, either through untrue beliefs or inaccurate concepts on the plane of the concrete mind, or through conditions prevailing on the physical plane, whether subjective or objective.

Principles of Esoteric Healing

You may, therefore, get a false concept preventing the life forces coming properly through the astral plane, or you may get the astral forces as instincts thwarted in their expression on the physical plane. You need to discern whether the thwarting is due fundamentally to opinions or to circumstances.

Whether, for instance, a man refrains from marriage owing to his religious opinions or his financial circumstances. The physical results will be the same, but the mental reactions will be widely different, and it is the mental reactions which become the physical results in another incarnation.

The etheric plane and the astral plane are best considered together for they are so intimately connected. Consider those cases in which the emotions are thwarted. Fear, dislike of uncongenial conditions, avoidance of unpleasantness, shirking of effort or responsibility, and unsatisfied desire, are the principal causes of subjective astral trouble. All these conditions tend to shut off the supply of vitality.

Remember that there are many cases in which, although there is no physical disease, the vitality is low. Fatigue comes on early; the subject is very susceptible to weather conditions; and in general has no resistance. Any emotional distress causes a further marked blocking of the vitality.

These cases are suffering from inhibitions in the astral body, and they must be dealt with psychologically.

Fear is best dealt with by teaching the patient means of protecting himself from that which he fears, which is by thought control and autosuggestion. The worry habit must also be counteracted by re-education.

The shirker is the most difficult. He desires to achieve his ends without paying the price. Dangle the carrot in front of the donkey's nose and use the whip on his hind-quarters. The shirker's self-esteem is the point of attack. Do not yourself

The Classification of Diseases

humiliate him, but so arrange matters that if he fails he humiliates himself.

In thwarted desire teach sublimation, power through sacrifice and reincarnation.

Trouble on the astral may be due to external causes, in the past or the present, such as astral interference from a knowledge of occultism and deliberate malpractice. Or it may be due to internal causes, such as deliberate distortion of the astral emotional forces through a thwarting of them. In the former case you will perceive displacement of the astral forces, which are often unduly strong. In the latter case there will be a shortage of vital force.

Such cases must be dealt with by mental healing. That is to say, the manipulation of thought forms by the trained mind of the operator, without the spoken word. Secondly, if the case is suitable, by a greater or lesser degree of teaching and reconstruction of the patient's outlook, and instruction in autosuggestion when once the principles have been acquired.

Never be content, however, with a purely material healing, because the patient is always liable to a relapse, or the outbreak of the old forces in a new form. That is to say, you may cure a man of kidney trouble only to see him develop a skin disease. Both being organs of elimination, the connection between the kidneys, and blood and the skin, is a very important one. Never feel that you have finished with a case until a spiritual healing has also taken place, and that person is harmonised with his Higher Self and the Cosmos.

The study of astral disease is a very large subject. It is intimately connected with all forms of endocrine diseases. Endocrine diseases are all astral in origin.

It is on this plane that we find in our practical work the most fruitful causes of the life forces becoming aberrant for various reasons; and it is more usual to find the astral plane

Principles of Esoteric Healing

affecting the mental plane in the majority of people rather than vice versa.

You have, on the astral or emotional plane, the meeting place of influences from various sources — from the spiritual plane even, because that level and the emotional have an affinity with each other. It is affected by the mental level, and it is also very strongly affected by the instincts.

It is also the plane of magic, so called, which simply means the manipulation of the astral and etheric forces. Here force is very free flowing, which is why it can be manipulated by those who know how. That is the work of the priest physician, and it is also his task to show the patient how he can control his own forces himself, which when done according to Cosmic Law, is the only permanent cure or way of health.

Astral disease — which we might rather call disharmony — manifests as symptoms on the etheric level. The astral plane is that which influences the etheric. Therefore with etheric conditions we must ask if they originate on the etheric plane, or are caused from the astral plane above.

It is the plane of vitality which is affected by astral disharmony. It is there that you have either too much force or too little, or unevenly distributed. And again, astral disharmony or disease can be caused by the plane below. It is when the instincts are not flowing freely that emotional disharmony results.

Emotional disharmony can also be produced from the mental plane, but it does not always originate from here so much as pass through, as when a soul is out of harmony with the source of its being, and spiritual maladjustment manifests as astral disharmony.

The emotional level being the meeting house of the forces from below and above, it is more often a question of disharmony rather than disease, except in cases of obsessional

52

The Classification of Diseases

origin, and here one can truly talk of astral disease. In diagnosing an astral disease note that it usually manifests in the form of an endocrine unbalance (although of course an endocrine unbalance may have a purely physical origin) or in functional nervous disorders, though in the latter case the trouble probably originates on the mental level first, which in turn upsets the astral.

Where do you think the astral body gets its food from? It gets its food in polarity. It gets it from another astral body by polarity. It gets it from the Earth itself, from sunlight, from the Moon forces and also from vegetation. And those forces build and work upon the etheric body.

But just as it is through the etheric that the physical assimilates, so it is through the astral that the etheric assimilates. And through the mental the astral assimilates, and through the spiritual the mental.

Diseases of the Mental Plane

We will next briefly consider the diseases of the mental level in man. There are three types: the organic, the poisons, and the vital diseases.

It is necessary to determine what is likely to go wrong with the life forces on this level in order to decide the method of treating it. First consider those disorders originating on the mental level itself and not those from the emotional level which so often affect it. You have here the realm of the distortions of the life force caused by inaccurate ideas — ideas which do not correspond to Cosmic realities. These inaccurate ideas lead to unbalance corresponding to the different Sephiroth according to their nature and produce overplus in some and deficiency in others.

We consider mainly in our therapeutic work the seven centres on the central pillar of the Tree of Life. The Sephiroth

Principles of Esoteric Healing

on the side pillars are also of importance, particularly in diagnosis, but the effects of these side pillars will be mainly expressed through the central centres with which they are intimately connected.

For example, the effects would be experienced in Daath of unbalance in the Sephiroth of Geburah and Chesed, because these two side Sephiroth unite in a third for functional purposes. That is why, in esoteric diagnosis, you do not only consider that which has visible effect, but you look around to the allied Sephiroth also. These are the general principles of diagnosis in all the four worlds, not only in the mental world.

Certain faulty mental viewpoints affect the centre or Sephirah to which they correspond. For instance, religious fanaticism when carried to the point of bigotry would be ascribed to Tiphareth, but it would tend towards its adverse aspect and cause lack of functioning in that Sephirah.

Another example would be over-conservatism, when carried to the point of excess, corresponding to Chesed. I am referring to the mental qualities of these vices and virtues which bring about the emotional after effects. Usually it is the other way around but in rarer cases the fundamental attitude is first there. When it is inaccurate and not founded on reality it produces psychopathologies, delusions, and so on.

The treatment for pathologies of the mental level is mainly psychological — that which is current in the world. You should also try to help the patient from the plane above, that is, you should help him to see the spiritual priniciple which is true and which should, when worked down to his problem on the level which is concerned, bring truth also into his mental world. Truth is the great standard on this level.

The Classification of Diseases

Poisoning and Sepsis

There are classes of disease, families of them, which go together. It is already recognised that asthma, hay fever and nettle rash are of the same family. Let me tell you of another — certain types of bladder trouble. There is an internal irritation as well as an external, and there are many complaints which belong to that family but have not been placed there.

Take those types of disease which are characterised by irritability of tissue. Can you not see it in the heart? They are of the same family, and that will give you a clue to a good many things if you think it out. Irritability of tissue is not always due to an infection.

There are two sorts of poisonings in the body — the poisons bred by foreign organisms, and the poisons bred by the secretions therein.

Think, for instance, when there is a reaction to a particular type of protein. You will be able to trace the origin of the subtlety of protein shock which has been successfully overcome, but the burnt child dreads fire, and the tissue which has to fight for its life sometimes turns on the defensive. Now you see how you get sensitive conditions. There is a traumatic origin, and subsequent shock, and the subsequent diseases are caused by the nervous reaction of the tissues concerned.

Take nettle rash. That has its origin in a poison which the tissues had to eliminate speedily. That particular type of poison, whenever the tissues meet the substance again, try to eliminate it in a hurry.

Two factors are required to produce the pathological reaction. When the breathing or skin surface are both affected, there may be that particular poison present whose presence

Principles of Esoteric Healing

alone would not produce the reaction. There must be poison plus emotion. Poison and no emotion — no reaction.

The usual method of purification resorted to is by the alimentary canal. Try the kidneys. Energise the activity of the kidneys and you will more speedily eliminate the poison which is poisoning the skin through the intestines. A case of "close the door after the horse has been stolen."

I may tell you further — it is not in the blood but in the lymphatic system that you get poisons.

Whenever you get an auto-intoxication, cleanse through the kidneys as well as through the bowels. Remember that the sweat glands of the skin and the cells of the kidneys are of very similar structure, and are very similar in their physiological activities, and the same astro-etheric system controls them both. The skin and kidneys go together, and they are eliminating organs of the same type. They are very closely allied.

I will tell you another pair of centres — the reproductive organs and the throat.

You should make a close study of the ductless glands, they are very important in your work. Long continued emotional conditions affect the ductless glands, and if in previous lives you have had long continued and powerful emotions, they will manifest in this life. This will explain many congenital diseases in this life.

Absence or partial absence of thyroid gland will always point to a definite acute terror, and with the psychic aspect forms the relation of a soul incarnating in a physical body. Many a thyroidal infant probably died of fright — of sheer terror, and you cannot be surprised at that soul being reluctant to incarnate.

The Classification of Diseases

And remember that the manner of the last death profoundly influences the attitude of the soul toward its physical body. Now the man who has died a natural death, gently sleeping as it were, comes back with a very healthy attitude towards his physical body, and so does the man who is killed by a sudden accident in the prime of his life. These are both healthy deaths, and those souls never think of themselves as sick.

Some people think of themselves as well, however ill they are. They look upon health as normal, and they are surprised at illness. Others look upon ill health as normal, and accept it as part of the normal way of living. These are the souls who died of a septic type. A bad sepsis sinks into the soul, it goes further than the physical plane.

You see, sepsis is a living organism. It has got a mind side. Mind will poison mind. The mass effect of a large number of living organisms affects the mind; and there is a group soul which affects the soul of the patient. Hence the temperamental change which takes place with a sepsis, and a change towards a different type of mentality in a profound specific poisoning.

If you understand the evolution of a bacterial species, you will know that parasites are against the law. Saprophytes are what they were meant to be. They break the law and become parasites, and the entities which control the different species of disease. They ought to have gone into limbo long ago, but they are planet-bound; they are vampires of their kind.

Take what happens when a whole class of life is being withdrawn, because evolution goes on, it goes to its sleep and must await the return of the cycle. If souls cannot evolve at the same pace they have to withdraw from the Earth and wait for the next arc. They are called the stragglers. The same thing applies to species — to types of life. Certain types of unicellular organism that should have evolved, fail to keep

Principles of Esoteric Healing

up; they dragged behind. And some of them, instead of waiting on the next planet for the phase to which they belong, become vampires.

It is not possible to do our form of therapeutic work except in a place in which we can make our mental atmosphere. Just as the surgeon must have his conditions, so must the psychologist. On the plane of the life forces it is the mental atmosphere which is your principal means of therapy, and that you make with the trained mind. For if you can give a sick soul hope and peace, you have gone a very long way towards restoring the vital forces, and it is on the question of directed vitality that you will work.

The function of physical medication is to remove obstructions from the path of vitality, and to provide the needed raw materials for its processes. Do you see the principle? The chief obstruction to vitality is sepsis — the invasion of an alien and destructive form of life.

The micro-organisms which produce disease are of the same nature as Earth-bound souls. They should have passed away in the course of evolution, but they are clinging to incarnation by living on living beings. It is not the Cosmic Law that the lower should feed on the higher. Parasitic forms of life are contrary to Cosmic Law. Apart from mechanical injury — trauma — your chief problems on the physical plane are those rebels against Cosmic Law, and deficiency diseases — infection and deficiency.

There is an entity to each type of disease. It has a distinct personality. If you get sporadic cases they are nothing but links. The virulence is most marked during an epidemic. The more you congregate the victims, the more virulent the manifestation. They know this in fever hospitals; that is why they always disinfect thoroughly and keep a ward free. They allow

The Classification of Diseases

the ground to lie fallow for a period. You will see then most typical examples in epidemics.

There is a great deal more in tuberculosis than we have considered. It has a very large aspect in the soul in which it grows. There is a very large predisposing element in it. You never get it in a single life for it is invariably a karmic disease. But there are other diseases, such as scarlet fever, smallpox and plague, which are infectious. A person is not liable to tuberculosis unless he has a rapport. There is no karmic aspect in scarlet fever. That is where you will see the clear cut examples to which I have referred.

Tuberculosis is really a disease of the etheric body, and unless that body is diseased to begin with, the disease will not develop in the physical body. It is essentially a disease of low resistance. That is why sunshine is so important. It always starts in the etheric, and healing always starts in the etheric. Now you see why the tissues break down — the etheric mould is damaged.

Principles of Esoteric Healing

4.
ESOTERIC DIAGNOSIS

First Principles of Esoteric Diagnosis

You must realise that the first principle in making a diagnosis, which must always precede treatment, is to begin by getting yourself in a particular state of mind.

That you will learn to do by daily meditation practice of it, because you have got to go back to the beginning of things, and there, in the remote past, pick up the trail, following it down the planes of manifestation, from the subtle to the dense, till you see where it turned off and became aberrant.

In order to do this you practise daily certain forms of meditation, because your own consciousness is the instrument you have to use. You are going to use your own reactions as diagnostic instruments. You go back to the source of life, or more correctly speaking, of force, for force is life and life is force. There is no distinction between spirit and matter except in the degree of activity and organisation. And so you commence your work by going back to the beginning of things and contemplating First Becoming.

That is not easy, and we do it by glyph and symbol. You want to study these and learn to use your mind in a particular way which enables it to think of remote things. And you do this as it has always been done — not with reason but with imagination.

Begin by seeing movement in space — the darkness of primordial night — the Rings and the Rays swinging into being and light beginning to glow as space moves into activity, and the dawn of another day of manifestation begins. *[Note: A more or less complete formula and sequence for this kind of*

Principles of Esoteric Healing

*meditation is contained in Dion Fortune's **Cosmic Doctrine**, which has been described as serving "to train the mind as much as to inform it."Ed.]*

What you contemplate you touch. What you enter into in imagination, you make yourself one with. For there is that in you and in all men, the Divine Spark we call it, which comes forth from the Fire of God; and that Divine Spark is not of this order of being but of the Unmanifest, which is beyond your comprehension.

And when you reach up thus, going out to the limits of existence, that Spark in you wakes into activity and something begins to happen in your soul, and there comes an awareness which cannot be put into words, but you are made one with all Being. And from there you start your diagnosis by putting yourself into a particular state of consciousness.

You may not understand this fully at present, but you will when you begin to experience it. Until you experience it, I can no more tell you what it is than I can describe light to a blind man. By practice you learn to get into this state of consciousness and rouse to activity the pure Cosmic Fire which is the core of your being. Then your mind changes its mode of thinking and you gain realisation and insight.

Start from that point, the beginning of life; come down in contemplation through the phases of manifestation and organisation of force into form, from the remote past down the ages and down the planes. It is simply and quickly done once you understand the nature of these things.

You bring your mind down the planes and approach the physical plane, not objectively from below upwards as in empirical science, but subjectively from above, coming down as if you set out with God upon the Path of Evolution.

Proceeding thus, you will finally come down to the physical plane, where your training has made you familiar with

Esoteric Diagnosis

matter, but with an insight which you will not have if you work from below upwards.

It is done to effect a change in your powers of perception; it is the method of the sacred science. We use the soul of man as an instrument of precision. You make yourself something and work with what you have made.

A healer has trained hands and can feel what the untrained person cannot feel. Can you explain this? So equally, you train your mind to perceive life at its source and you will understand the processes of disease and their diagnosis. And in the light of what you know, treatment can be applied.

When you have learnt how to let your mind unfold from the beginning of things, coming down into matter, not thinking in words but in pictures, you will have learnt the first stage of the technique.

Begin by visualising the dark primordial night; see the light beginning to glow and the Rays shining out. There is a tradition in these things. The mind is poised and supplied with sufficient data; that is how the sacred science is worked out. The ancients trusted the powers of the equilibrated mind before instruments were invented; they knew many things now proved by modern science.

When you have learnt the practice of building evolution in imagination from dark space down to organised matter, you can apply what you know to the individual patient.

To do this, first put yourself in a suitable frame of mind. Then call up the image of the patient — not the disease, but his personality. See through to the heart of the man. See the spiritual nucleus within him, and raise your consciousness to the First Beginning.

Take with you the image of the Divine Spark which symbolises the man, and which on that plane is just a spark,

Principles of Esoteric Healing

and follow in your imagination down the planes the evolution of that immortal being, and you will understand then, with insight, the nature of the problems that man is working out in this life, and the life and the causes that have made him what he is. You will then come to that man with profound insight of his life, and you will diagnose his problems for him at an altogether deeper level than you could if you approached them objectively from the physical plane alone. That is the basis of the method I teach, if you wish to learn it.

The first mode of approach is always along the line of evolving life. The second is to make of yourself the instrument which you use. That is the practical side of the work. It depends on natural aptitude.

You may find it easy, or some perhaps have no aptitude. It depends on what you bring to the work. You may find it quite easy, or you may find it one of those things that, only when you try, you find that you can do.

You work on yourself through visual imagination, and that brings intuition to a fine focus. Intuition is mind working beyond forms. If you learn to carry consciousness beyond the normal, intuition and reason join up together.

You learn to carry consciousness beyond the normal by use of symbolism, which is the algebra of the mind. When you have learnt to do this, you can discard the symbol, which is like the scaffolding on a building, but a very useful scaffolding.

When you have grasped these principles, then you will be able to apply them to the practical work. You will find that it has a remarkable effect on your mind. Consciousness will extend and grow in a way not yet realised. Study along these lines. Study the old traditions on which men have been trained for thousands of years, but proceed one step at a time.

Esoteric Diagnosis

First train your mind so that you can get a realisation of the higher levels of being and feel yourself one with life, and then life will teach you. You will see with clear sight, for that is what you need first for diagnosis. Then comes the understanding of your own self. The priesthood of medicine pursue a sacred science, not to be taught or understood by the profane.

Life is God made manifest and is sacred, and unless you have respect for life in a man you cannot approach him by this method. For it is the deeper healing, not only of the body, but of the soul itself which builds the body, and in building may go astray.

Life can become aberrant at different levels, and according to where it leaves the true line will be the point where you seek the root of the cause. Below that you will deal with secondary causes and finally with effects.

The same conditions seen in matter may have originated at different levels. Sometimes they go far back. Sometimes they are near at hand. Learn to follow the train of evolving life and try to see where it departed from equilibrium and normality.

It is not wise to apply this teaching at first to anyone but yourself. Learn to use the method in meditation until you can see these things clearly. When you can lose yourself in the beginnings of creation you can begin to follow the trail. Make haste slowly. Allow time in these matters. Do not try to hasten the hatching of the egg by boiling it.

These are the principles of esoteric diagnosis, and it is now necessary to describe some particular applications of those principles. It is only when applications have been made on the physical plane, even if only in token and partial form through lack of opportunity or knowledge, that any real realisation of these principles can take place. And until such

Principles of Esoteric Healing

realisations have taken place, you will not fully understand the implications and applications of those principles.

Your work must manifest in your daily life. You must be a Healer Priest or Priestess, and that is something which you should be all the time, and that is very much more than any intellectual appreciation of principles. You must learn to apply these principles, even though imperfectly — for a beginning must be made. You are your own instrument and it is necessary to perfect that instrument. It is a gradual process, but only attained by making a beginning and trying.

In esoteric diagnosis it is essential to have the development of the intuitive faculty. Also important, though not so much, is the visual clairvoyant faculty, because a clairvoyant faculty will show you on the inner planes the conditions of what things are, but not necessarily the interpretation thereof — because that is on the plane above, the plane of causes.

Development of the Intuitive Faculty

You must develop your intuitions, because, for the practical application of the teaching, it is essential that this power should be achieved. Until these teachings have been actually applied upon the physical plane, they cannot be said to have fully come through, or to have spread in any way to the Group Soul. That is why you must first learn to develop yourself in order to be able to apply the teaching.

Always regard your patients from the viewpoint of evolving life. When once you have, and can maintain the correct viewpoint in connection with your patients' condition, which is seeing them whole, as a soul working through the machinery of vehicles, then all specific points in connection thereto will fall into relative place.

66

Esoteric Diagnosis

The intuitive factor increases with use. Many physicians use it although they do not understand it or what it is, and are unable to give it a name.

As in meditation, if you wish to obtain enlightenment upon a symbol you meditate upon it, and let what images and associations thereto rise up. For the intuitive approach, you contemplate the patient, rather than using the more concentrated attention as in the psychic type of diagnosis, because you are trying to catch the fleeting impressions from your own higher consciousness relative to the patient.

Practice is necessary in the development of intuitional perception. Though you may think this a very obvious remark, it is true nevertheless. You will find it is helpful to try and develop your intuitions by a method which can be counterchecked, because thereby you will gain added confidence and faith, and faith is necessary.

Method 1

When you come to consider one of your patients — it may not always be practicable — try to make your intuitive diagnosis first, if possible writing down any impressions you gain without any physical examination at all. Then examine your patient in the ordinary way, and afterwards see whether any of your impressions have been corroborated or no.

Of course the physical examination will only corroborate or otherwise an intuitive diagnosis appertaining to the physical plane, but intuitions can be applied to the physical plane as well as to the inner plane conditions, and by this means you can check your conclusions, and you should persevere with this.

Do not attach too much importance to one case only, but continue with many and do not be disheartened by lack of

Principles of Esoteric Healing

results. Of course, when you come to your physical examination, naturally you must set aside any preconceived ideas you may have provisionally made and proceed objectively. It would be better to confine this practice with your patients to the physical level until you have gained facility.

Method 2

You can also practice your intuitive powers upon the conditions of those people with whom you are in contact around you. Needless to say this should be done with discretion. But even here, where your intuitive deductions apply to the subtler planes, there is to some extent a means of counterchecking. You can wait on events, and sooner or later they will show you whether your intuitions were correct or not; but you may have to wait some time for corroboration.

Method 3

Direct intuitional perception can be helped by giving attention to the finer shades of emanations from a person, from which you can pick up their condition. When you want to sense a person's condition you should deliberately and under control unfold your aura, so that you receive the subtle impressions, and can then intepret them.

This must be done under control, clearly distinguishing between what comes from outside and your own reactions, and closing down afterwards, so that you do not carry this around all the time, which would be injurious. Similarly with other forms of work, particularly when power is used, the aura would be closed to outside impressions.

Method 4

When examining a patient, although at the time you may be concerned with a purely physical diagnosis, if you consider

Esoteric Diagnosis

him later, trying to put yourself mentally en rapport with him, you may gauge something of his condition, and make some attempt to form a real and complete diagnosis as to why such a disease manifested, going back to original and fundamental causes, which may not be on the physical plane at all.

This is a matter of experience, and success only comes gradually and with constant attempts, but unless you try to form some esoteric diagnosis as well as the purely physical, you are not giving yourself the benefit of experience on these lines. The first attempts may be imperfect and cause you to think that you are not getting results.

Method 5

The Pineal Centre is the seat of the intuitive sense, and lies in the forehead over the nose. When you are seeking to assess the minds of your patients, look at them from this third eye. Listen intuitively to the mind of your patient. Listen as well as look. Watch the mental pictures rise in your own mind by the sympathetic induction of vibration; and when you have concluded, cut the rapport between you and your patient by visualising your hand with a sharp knife in it and draw that knife between you and your patient, cutting in front of the centres of the forehead and the solar plexus.

Intuitional perception and the Higher Self

You must remember above all that it is from the Higher Self that intuition is derived, and therefore whatever you do to hasten and bring about the process of the integration of your Higher and Lower Selves, will enable you more quickly to develop these powers.

It is vitally necessary to develop these powers before much practical advance can be made in esoteric healing, because

Principles of Esoteric Healing

that is what distinguishes a Healer Priest from an exoteric physician. It is not merely a greater theoretical knowledge of certain little understood causes and conditions, but by the power of the Higher Self functioning through the personality, being able to bring these forces to bear, after intution has first shed light upon the conditions with which one is dealing.

So there is a twofold process involved:

a) acquiring the knowledge and teaching that will enable you to apply your powers when you so develop them, and

b) the training and development of yourself, which is the first necessity for their practical application.

However, at the same time, the attempt to use these intuitive powers is one of the ways in which the Higher Self can be brought down.

The technique to be used in maintaining contact with the Higher Self is that taught in the Western Mystery Tradition, which is to concentrate the forces when one wants them and to close down afterwards. It is not possible continuously to maintain very close connection with the Higher Self, though in a sense its aims and aspirations can so impress themselves on the personality that they will become an automatic reaction. The discipline of meditation will help. Concentrate on getting your contacts once a day and you will keep the channels open.

Development of the Clairvoyant Faculty

Clairvoyance is a development of the powers of visualisation. Visualisation can be what you yourself build to express an idea or a picture. It is really the symbolisation of certain forces.

Conversely, the forces picked up by the mechanism of the psyche are clothed in the symbolism of pictures, and you can deduce the forces from the pictures. This faculty must

Esoteric Diagnosis

be exercised in the same way as you exercise the intuitional faculty. Experience can be achieved by taking note of and recording your inner visual impressions.

The Pineal Centre corresponds in evolution to the development of a level of consciousness corresponding to the development of physical structure. Upon the Tree of Life it is correlated with Daath, and in man it is situated in the triangle between the brows at the base of the nose. If you were to look with clairvoyant vision as the pineal centre is opening up, you would see a disc of light in front of the centre of the forehead. It is the seat of the intuitive sense.

To visualise the Etheric Double and the Aura it is necessary to develop your pineal centre. To obtain a clear vision you combine the physical eye with the third eye and the astral.

To see the Etheric Double, look at a patient so that your focus is just behind him. When the body is out of focus it will have a blurred edge. Let your eyes focus a yard behind him. Try not to look at the body, but watch that blurred edge out of the corner of your eye, and then you will find that the third eye will be able to perceive the etheric condition.

The physical eyes look at the person a yard out of focus. You will obtain the third eye by direct attention at the base of the nose, until you feel a slight quiver. Then allow the imagination to perceive that misty outline. You see then, not only the etheric, but also the astral aura.

The etheric double is colourless, the aura is coloured. The etheric is of gaseous substance, like smoke. Watch for it systematically. For visualising the aura it is very helpful to see the patient against a dark blue background — the colour of the sky by night.

You can try visualisation of physical organs with the astral eye. Look at a patient and imagine that you see his heart.

Principles of Esoteric Healing

Note its appearance. Watch it working. Concentrate on it. Watch it and let the image rise.

See what you can see, and then confirm by stethoscope or X-ray. In that way you will learn to observe organs with the astral eye.

The significance of the Etheric Double

The etheric aura indicates the physical diseases of the patient and shows the general condition of health. It may be standing out from the patient, or flaccid as in ill-health where the general vitality is lowered.

It also shows the area of diseased organs, sometimes when the physical is still apparently normal, for when the disease originates on the upper levels, it is the etheric counterpart which is affected before the disease is manifested on the physical body.

Equally, when a disease originates in the physical, for example trauma, the etheric will not be immediately affected, unless the condition becomes chronic, when the blockage of vitality will cause that area to show up.

Usually the etheric aura has a darker colour in disease than in health.

Thought forms

There is a difference between thought forms and astral entities. Thought forms may be generated by a patient or projected from another mind. Astral entities may be rapports or elementals and will be dealt with later, under Rapports. Astral entities are very much larger than thought forms. They can be anything from a couple of feet to twenty to thirty feet in dimension.

Esoteric Diagnosis

When using your pineal centre to visualise the aura, behind that aura you will see a continual movement of shadowy forms, some inch or two across. These are the thought forms as they appear to astral sight, and in that medley you will be able to pick out some of a different outline to the others, and these will be coloured according to ray type.

For practical therapeutic purposes look for the red, the indigo and the green ones.

The red indicate the positive passions.

The indigo indicate repressions.

The green are usually concerned with the positive aspects maladapted, and strictly speaking are not pathological.

Pick up one of these thought forms and focus on it. Let it stand out. Enlarge that thought form, and let it present a picture to you. Let is assume the image in imagination, until you see it clearly. Then having seen it, banish it; you do not want it in your aura.

When the thought forms derive from a patient they are seen in his aura, and may appear about the size of your fist until they are enlarged.

When thought forms are projected from another mind, you do not find them in the aura but outside the aura, surrounding it. If you are so fortunate as to observe at a time when they are being projected, you will see them coming out of the distance.

If you concentrate on a patient's forehead between his eyes you will be able to read his conscious thoughts. If you concentrate about six inches to a yard behind a patient you will be able to get impressions of his subconscious thought.

For that which is hidden from consciousness you must concentrate behind the spine — you will get an impression of atmospheric conditions but no details. You get the background of consciousness by examining the rear side of the aura.

Principles of Esoteric Healing

You get at the Higher Self of a patient by concentrating on the aura over the head. The higher consciousness is in the aura over the head, not in the head. It never coincides with the physical body.

Practical Applications

Diseases may be divided, for all practical purposes, into those which originate above and work downwards, and those which originate below and work upwards. When making your diagnosis your first care should be to find the point at which the dis-harmony originated, both in time and space.

That is to say, you must discern the plane to which the cause should be assigned. You should then discern whether it originates with this incarnation or in the immediate past, (that is, within three incarnations) or in the remote past.

For instance, Epilepsy, unless caused by some gross injury to the nervous system in this incarnation, may be found to be due to dabbling with magic in the past. I use the word dabbling advisedly, because it is not a misfortune to which the expert magician is liable, but characterises those who invoke power they cannot control. In dealing with epilepsy you have to consider the possibility of relationship between that person and external occult forces, and the mental operations should be those of purification and protection. You may find that the epilepsy originated on the astral plane anything from four to seven incarnations away. You also need to distinguish between those diseases which are due to the errors of the patient and those of which he is the innocent victim.

Obsession may or may not be his own fault. It is very important to get a true diagnosis on this point, and to see whether the patient has brought about his own trouble or is an innocent victim. This is because, in this type of therapeutic work, you have to enlist the voluntary and intelligent co-operation

Esoteric Diagnosis

of your patient, and if his disease is innocently acquired, protection and the breaking of the rapport are all that is needed. But if it was developed through his own errors, far reaching construction of character may be necessary, and in all cases you have to judge how much explanation you can give to your patient. Much of your work must be done silently by the influence of the unspoken thought and the power of trained mental work.

In these teachings we are giving principles, and trying to inculcate an attitude of mind towards the problems of medicine. Given principles, and the mental method of approach, you can work out the application for yourself.

Correspondences

In general terms when considering factors (not necessarily diseased ones) affecting the personality, you should observe that personality as it really is.

Without using intuitive or clairvoyant powers some insight may be obtained by appraising how much certain personality traits are really so much established that they are part of that personality — which you cannot easily visualise the person being without — and that which gives the impression of being an addition.

For example, you might have a child who was naturally of a fearless, spirited disposition — that was its native temperament. Yet if it had some terrible experience, its spirit might have been so affected that it would appear a very nervous and timid child. But there would be a subtle difference between it and the child who was timid and fearful temperamentally.

By analogy, the same thing applies when considering past lives. Of that which is built right into the personality you

75

Principles of Esoteric Healing

might look to past lives for its causation. That which seems rather grafted on, and perhaps in some way not fitting the rest of the personality, you may suspect to be of recent origin. As you may know, chronic cases are hard to cure, and that is even more so the case when it is a chronic case dating back to other lives.

There is a direct correlation between the vehicle that is diseased in this life and that of a previous life. Man being four-fold by nature — spirit, mind, emotion and body — disharmony in the sphere of the mind will affect the mental vehicle. And if continued, will affect those below it, working down the planes to the emotional and etheric. So the etheric will eventually be affected by disharmony long continued in a past life, though that disharmony might have originated at any level.

That is why the physical disease manifests in another life, because the Ghost carries the seed atom of this etheric framework. So although the etheric body of a past life is the direct causative factor of an illness in this life, through the present etheric body, nevertheless that body is not necessarily the original cause, which might lie many planes above it.

As in this life disordered life forces can work down the planes to affect the physical; the same thing can have happened in a past life. To get to the real cause, you must find out what caused the etheric effect in that past life. And here, in terms of the vehicles, it is generally to the mental or emotional levels you will have to look.

It is true that the instincts, which are on the etheric level, can produce disharmony. But if that takes place it is always linked with the emotional or mental factor. Animals do not suffer from repressions and distortions of their instincts, because they have not the mental and emotional factors which deflect them. So from a practical diagnostic point of view look to the emotional or mental level for a primary cause in a past

Esoteric Diagnosis

life when considering a disease which has originated from a past life.

The diseased organ in a particular life does not indicate the cause, because the same disease or symptoms can have many causes, though manifesting as the same disease in different patients. It can have a specific bearing when considered in relation to other factors, but not primarily. Make your individual diagnosis first and then for additional light think of the correspondence.

To some extent there is a correspondence in a general way, in that certain parts of the body are associated with certain levels of consciousness, these correspondences being according to the Microcosmic Tree of Life. But in considering an individual patient there is the factor of his previous life conditions, and his physical make up through the medium of the etheric body, which is the mould for the physical, and hence he may have a weakness in a particular place.

Take two patients. Both, say, may have a similar subtle cause which is producing disharmony, but in working down to the physical body, the disease may attack each person in a different place. That is explained by their different past lives.

In the same way, two patients with the same disease may have quite different subtle causes producing that same disease. It might even be at different levels, perhaps one mental and the other emotional. That is where the true art of the physician comes in, because you cannot treat people by rule of thumb and apply a set formula just because the disease is the same on the physical plane.

Consider correspondences in relation to the Tree of Life. For example, co-ordination of the nervous system to Daath; and excretion to Malkuth. This is viewing the body from the point of view of function rather than anatomy, and it is with

Principles of Esoteric Healing

function that we are concerned. Ask what the organ under consideration does, and then ascribe it.

The seven centres correlate with the central pillar of the Tree of Life, and in making these correlations from an anatomical point of view you must consider the function of the organs in relation to the Tree rather than having a geometrically tidy system. The human body is not exactly geometrical.

Of diseases that have a past origin, you can include all congenital diseases, diseases of an obsessional nature such as cancer, and those in which the etheric has been previously damaged, such as epilepsy.

Concerning diseases originating in the present life, we cannot, except in a few cases, always ascribe a definite level of origination to a specific disease, because one disease may have been produced by different causes in different people.

5.
THERAPEUTIC METHODS

Relaxation and its Value

The art of relaxation, at will, is as necessary as the capacity to direct all one's energies to one point when required. One pointed concentration is an essential capacity in all mental work, but its antithesis is not sufficiently appreciated. It is not possible to continue concentration for very long periods, and unless one relaxes when the time so to do comes, there is an undue wear and strain on the system generally, leading to lessened capacity, when a further effort is required. The bow should not always be bent. It is a question of control — mental and emotional control — and the choice of the plane and the aspect on which one wishes to function.

This subject has great bearing on healing generally and upon endocrine balance. Many doctors tell their patients "Do not worry!" for it is well known that worry has an adverse effect upon their recuperation. But they do not know enough to tell their patient how to *prevent* worry.

The loss of mental relaxation plays a great part in endocrine unbalance. There is a perpetual and unnatural demand or strain on certain aspects of the patient's endocrine system. It may be emotional or mental worry reacting on the endocrines through the Centres, or it may be more indirect, through the close linking of the mind with the body.

In most people any mental strain tends to have its physical counterpart in muscular contraction. Consider the young child when learning to write. It perhaps frowns, and uses all its body in various forms of contortion whilst it endeavours to spell out the alphabet. The same thing occurs in adults, to a

Principles of Esoteric Healing

greater or lesser extent. This may not be so apparent if superficial control has been acquired but there is often a strain there. This strain upsets the equilibrium of the body when it is prolonged over a considerable period.

Relaxation, to be complete, must be on the Four Levels.

First relax all the physical muscles so that there is no strain or tension.

Then you must have quiet, calm and serenity of the emotions.

The mind, if it tends to be over active, is a potent source of tension and strain. It must be quietened.

And of course on the spiritual level there is harmony already.

This is a two-fold process. Relax the body, emotions and mind, to enable the tranquillising effect of the spiritual to come down.

Equally, help the relaxation of the lower levels by mystical meditation on principles.

This is a very useful way to quieten an over-active mind, because it is very difficult to deal with the concrete mind on its own level. Bring the abstract mind of ideals to quieten the strain and tension produced by the concrete mind.

Rhythmic breathing is a good method to use in relaxation, for it calms the emotions, and quietens the over-active brain. The attention that is required for maintaining the breathing at a slow and steady pace has a calming effect, and when proficiency is attained, it is helpful in making that transition to the higher types of meditation, because the rate of breathing is correlated very closely with the changes in consciousness.

Therapeutic Methods

Suggestion

Suggestion plays an enormous part in both health and disease, and upon it rested the very early attempts of healing methods.

In primitive times many healings were brought about by the natural recuperative forces of nature within the organism. And by the faith that the patient had in the medicine man or certain herbs or incantations he gave himself autosuggestion of a healing nature.

In ancient Greece in their healing temples great importance was attached to the Temple Sleep as a method of healing. The patients, after their long and strenuous journey, were placed for the night in a chamber in a certain part of the Temple. They would have prepared themselves beforehand with perhaps fasting and prayer, and during the night whilst asleep, the priests would approach with the sacred snake, sometimes touching their complaints or whispering methods of treatment to them. The patient might be still asleep or in a semi-somnolent condition, and on the following morning he would recount his dreams, which would be taken as a form of oracle appertaining to his condition.

At first sight these ancient healing methods may appear rather a superstitious practice without much avail. But if you consider the medicine of today, you can see that the same thing is happening but under a different guise. The type of suggestion has changed. No longer do people recite incantations, instead they believe in advertisements, perhaps not consciously but subconsciously. This again is a form of suggestion.

If you consider more closely the principles that were involved in these old healing arts, you will find certain factors present. The factors of suggestion, faith and some of the early beginnings of dream interpretation, which has come again to the fore in psycho-analysis. Thus many of the older treatments,

Principles of Esoteric Healing

when examined for the principles underlying them, will be found to have a sound basis, but their application varies from one age to another.

Thus you should bear in mind that certain principles — namely the power of suggestion on the human mind for healing or for harm — are true and persist through the ages. It is for you to find suitable means to clothe your suggestions. The medicine man of some tribe will have forms to convey suggestion which are suited to his type of patient. You must suit your suggestion to your patients, but this is an individual matter which will differ with each patient. It is very important to be careful what you say to a patient, whether it is true or not.

However, you must not go to the other extreme and tell the patient that everything is fine when it is not so. For by so doing it may have the contrary effect, and the patient will lose confidence in you and in the power of further suggestions that you may make to him. With some patients, indeed, it may be better to paint a black picture, if this makes them more inclined to believe in you and likely to follow your advice.

Thus suggestion is a definite therapeutic technique, often disguised as ordinary conversation. But it must be remembered that whatever a doctor says always acts on the patient as a suggestion, be it in a negative or positive way. Therefore choose carefully words which are helpful and not hindering. And remember that words of help to one may act in quite the opposite manner to another.

The same considerations apply to the patient's environment. It is often a bad policy to have a patient surrounded by his own family, for in many cases the form of suggestions around him is not helpful and can greatly hinder recovery. It is not so much what is said, but what the patient himself believes has been said, for it is reaction to what is said that counts.

Therapeutic Methods

Patent medicines have been known to have cured various diseases, and adherents swear by their own panacea. It is true that these medicines have been of help, but their real curative power lay in the fact that the patient really believed in their marvellous efficacy.

This suggestive power is well known in theory by the medical profession, but there is quite a technique in its administration. The coloured bottle of medicine is no longer effective in itself, it must be given with skill, for the reasoning faculties of the patient have now advanced. The specific medicine and the rationale of treatment can be explained to most patients, as it will give an added reason for believing that it will do them good, so that their own suggestive powers will act more strongly.

The use of suggestion is a definite method of treatment and is of great value, but to some extent special conditions are necessary. It is not one that the doctor in a general hospital can apply very easily in the course of his work, for it should be undertaken in a place where sympathy is held for such a form of treatment. However, mild forms can be used by a doctor with all his contacts with his patients as far as attitude is concerned, especially in trying to develop the will to recover, which is so often lacking. It can undoubtedly act more than as an auxiliary in treatment, and more use of it should be made than is done at present. In the sphere of functional diseases, suggestion as a therapeutic measure is of great value and it has been known to bring about healing, even when organic disease was present.

Suggestion must be used in enlisting the patient's own natural springs of healing within the depths of his own mind. In the very deepest levels of the physical body there is a Will to full healthy functioning. Treatment should be aimed to allow cooperation to take place at those very deep subconscious levels.

Principles of Esoteric Healing

This is a very important point, because if you gain your patient's co-operation on this level, it is not just a surface acquiescence. And it is on the patient's will to recover and by putting him in touch with his own curative forces within himself that healing is brought about. These forces are for ever working for health, and disease is often the effort to compensate for some disharmony.

Hope is one of the strongest medicines, but it has to be the genuine article. Glib assurances that "you are getting better" are useless. It must be real hope because then the patient is aligned with the evolutionary and regenerative forces. You know, of course, that all physical conditions cannot as yet be cured, but nevertheless, if you cannot give hope of physical recovery, then try and give your patient hope in the Good Law, whether he is going to die or remain ill, because then he can co-operate.

The principles of Christian Science are not completely sound, but it can be of benefit to some people. It is a question of the planes. On the spiritual plane there is no disease and all is harmonious, but unless a person can function on that plane, or have even subconscious faith in that plane that he really is perfect, results of a beneficial nature rarely occur. The patient may sometimes repeat the affirmations rather from the point of view of a consciously held belief than one of real faith. For real faith is a subconscious belief.

It is possible to bring about changes on the physical plane by means directed from the mental and spiritual levels, but this is a method which few can apply. Great good is often obtained in curing conditions arising from the emotional and mental levels, because in these cases the plane of spiritual aspiration contacted by the affirmation brings harmony, and hence healing, to those two planes. Of course only those of an uncritical mentality can accept all its tenets, and without complete acceptance the method will not work.

Therapeutic Methods

For those types in whom the emotional factor is stronger than the mental, where they go more upon the feeling of a situation than the facts, and also for the insane, where it is useless to approach them through the mind, subconscious suggestion is the most profitable method. You give this suggestion mentally in precisely the same way as it is given verbally. It is always necessary to deal in affirmations and not negations.

Tell the patient what is going to happen, not what might happen. At the same time as the purely mental suggestion is given to the patient, you will also find that emotional suggestion can to some extent be of help also. That is something that should emanate from the doctor all the time, for it is that which gives confidence to a patient.

For the more mental type of patient, who in many cases has quite an influence over his subconscious, according to what he believes, it is very necessary to give suggestion verbally by speech to his concrete mind. By his acceptance he will influence his own subconscious mind, and he will continue to do so after the doctor has left.

Hypnosis is but a form of deeply applied suggestion by another person, and could be used in refractory cases. After its use the patient should be taught the value of auto-suggestion.

The principle of auto-suggestion can be expressed as the combination of faith and the creative power of the imagination. This has a beneficial effect for the patient is not left with any feelings of dependence on the power of another but is taught to apply his own powers to himself, which is the way of all true permanent healing. The physician can but assist this process whereby the natural forces and powers of the patient will, ideally, keep him in health afterwards.

Principles of Esoteric Healing

Hypnosis

Hypnotism can be a very useful weapon in the armoury of the doctor, but it should never be considered as a treatment in itself. By hypnotism a control is exercised over the subconscious mind — often at a very deep level of the autonomic nervous system, where the pulse rate and respiratory rate and other processes can be influenced by the will of the operator.

Normally this control in health should be exercised by one's own subconscious mind. By hypnosis the physical condition can be rectified but there will be no permanent cure as the basic disharmony would still operate and in due course produce the same or another disease.

As drugs are justified in their usage for an acute malady, which if left to slower more natural means of treatment would cause death, so should hypnosis be used. It is a quick method of altering the functioning of an organism, especially on the subtler levels, but once this is corrected and the body is again in functional order, then psychological treatment should be given, or whatever is necessary in building up a new regime of life — for the patient will have neglected the law of his own being in some way or other and, if not corrected, ill health will again supervene.

Disease is nature telling us that something is wrong and this must be altered to conform with the laws of nature. For example, it is useless to treat for indigestion if the patient still persists in eating the wrong food. Thus a temporary cure is no use. It must be carefully followed up so that the patient does not continue along the same path of error.

Hypnosis is used for functional nervous diseases. Thus a pseudo-paralysed limb can be made to move. Always the prior cause must be dealt with. Hypnosis is very useful in some cases in eliciting and tracing back the source of a trouble, especially if of psychological trauma of early youth.

Therapeutic Methods

Hypnosis is essentially a first-aid treatment, never final. When the aetiology is deep-seated, for example, in the soul itself, the point of free-will will arise. Always the patient must learn the lesson and, unless this is done, it is harmful to remove the cause, as the evolutionary process would be inhibited.

These treatments always take time, and care must be taken to ensure that the patient strengthens himself by character development, etc., so that he may be more fitted to cope with his environment, especially if an emotional unbalance is present. In this way, the trouble may not recur if the ground is cleared, for more psychological maturity will have arisen in the meantime. Of course, this depends on the patient's degree of co-operation, for little can be done otherwise.

Functional paralysis is brought about by an affect upon the etheric counterpart of a particular organ. This counterpart is conditioned by the mental attitude of the patient and his subconscious desire, that is, not to use a particular limb. Thus there would be a stoppage in the free flow of vitality, causing a deadness in that etheric limb, which would then also affect the physical counterpart. In these cases, by re-activating the flow of etheric force over that area, there will ensue a return of feeling and motor power to the physical counterpart.

The distribution of the etheric forces wells up and spreads from the Centres over the whole body. In functional paralysis there is a deficiency of force, so the Centre requires stimulation. The ductless glands correlate with the Central Pillar of the Tree of Life. The Side Pillars in man have no specific correlation but they form the focussing point for etheric forces in the limbs. Etherically speaking, they are distribution centres. So, for example, if you were considering the leg and you concentrated on the side Centre of Hod or Netzach, it would be the focussing point for those forces. However, there is no exact parallel between a specific Centre and a limb.

Principles of Esoteric Healing

When considered in all its ramifications, hypnotism covers a very wide field — as wide as that covered by the field of the subconscious mind, because hypnotism opens up the field of the subconscious mind. Therefore, all that can be drawn from the subconscious mind of the subject is covered by the field of hypnosis. This can be done at will and selective aspects chosen, whereas in other methods, such as analysis, only certain portions can be laboriously drawn up to the light with the help of the analyst.

With the aid of hypnosis any aspect of the subconscious mind can be tapped. Perhaps any aspect is too broad a term, as it would depend on the operator. If the operator were of a lower stage of spiritual realisation than the subject he could only draw forth to the limit of his own realisations.

Results in hypnotism are always possible unless prior auto-suggestion has been made by the patient either consciously or subconsciously, but on the more mental levels of the subconscious the results obtained by psycho-analysis are better and more lasting, because an integration of consciousness and subconsciousness is obtained.

There are different levels of the subconscious mind. The deeper levels correlate with the animal, vegetable and even mineral levels of existence. The more superficial belong to the emotional and the thinking processes which are no longer conscious.

The aim of the hypnotist, when dealing with the flow of vitality, is to by-pass the thinking in order to free the emotional. This is done by holding a clear mental picture of the correct condition within the body and then stating that the vitality is flowing to such and such an organ or area, if deficiency is present, or, if congested, that it is flowing evenly and freely. The flow of vitality answers to the will of the hypnotist.

Therapeutic Methods

The power of the inner planes, acting through a channel, produces a light hypnosis in the subject. Hypnosis varies from a very slight state of attention on the part of the patient to the very deepest trance condition, and, as hypnotism covers the whole sphere of the subconscious mind, this also includes the superconsciousness, as it is called, which is part of the subconscious.

This attention, or form of hypnosis, lulls the mind — the reasoning surface mind of the subject, which is the least part, and often but a barrier — and that enables the forces to be more easily contacted. It is always a two-way process because there has to be that response from the subject which enables one to proceed further.

In one sense it is hypnotism but it is really in no way imposing one's will upon the subject because that level can only be contacted when a reply is elicited, however slight. But when that is done it is like the small trickle through a sluice which becomes a stream, and that level you can help and open out by the power flowing through.

Hypnotism, sleep and dreams are allied subjects because they all concern the workings of the subconscious mind. Hypnotism is derived from the Greek word "hypnos" which means sleep. In natural sleep the normal physiological reflex action brought about by fatigue and by the accumulation of toxins in the bloodstream brings about the cessation of the conscious mind and hence the free functioning of the subconscious. In hypnotism the sleep-like condition is produced by artificial fatigue and dulling of the conscious mind.

Normal sleep can be used by a person to produce some of the effects which are produced under hypnotism by an operator — namely the effects produced by auto-suggestion — which is carried on and is worked upon by the subconscious and during the period of sleep. This is why it is recommended

Principles of Esoteric Healing

that auto-suggestion should be done during that drowsy period preceding sleep.

In the treatment of certain mental diseases continuous sleep is produced by the administration of drugs, so that the rest given the patient enables his nervous system and his mental functioning to recuperate and return to some degree of normality. This sleep might be better done as hypnotic sleep, as then the body would not have to contend with the drug itself and the unfavourable reactions to it afterwards.

Certain forms of mental disease are produced by pressure of circumstances and environment upon the mental and physical organism of a person, and every individual varies in his reactions and his nervous system, and either an inherent weakness or a piling up of things leading to the "last straw" may bring about a mental collapse.

Once the nervous system is built up — which is done by the deeper levels of the subconscious — then, on awakening, with strengthened nervous system he can cope with his environment. This breaks the vicious circle and gives him a chance. Whether the cure is permanent or not will depend on the fundamental cause. If due to an inherent mental condition which is left uncorrected then the same cause will bring about the same condition again. But if the symptoms were only brought about by outside pressure of circumstances, then the cure may be permanent, when the patient is given a chance.

During sleep there is a reversal of polarity between the vehicles; the physical body becomes negative and the deeper levels and the Inner Planes positive to it. When awake, the reverse is true in ordinary people. This factor has some part in the healing produced in the sleeping state, as the influence of the Higher Self upon the Lower Self is always of a healing and harmonious nature. Remember that it is the "magical bodies" that carry imperfections. Higher Selves can be developed only to a very limited degree in some people, but they

Therapeutic Methods

are perfect as far as they go, because, being composed of the three upper levels of the planes, they contain no imperfections in themselves.

Vitality

With regard to the therapeutic aspect of esoteric medicine your work lies where body and mind meet. You will be dealing with cases where the mental factor is affecting the physical conditions, and cases where the physical factor is affecting mental conditions. It is on the cusp of the planes that you will need to work.

The mind acts on the body through the ductless glands and the nerve controlling system; and the body acts on the mind through the chemical composition of the blood. Whatever affects the chemical composition of the blood affects brain consciousness in the expression of the ego upon the physical plane. Always remember that the point where the body contacts its subtle aspects is the endocrine system. Study that.

A big advance of medicine in the future could be in the study of vitality. Vitality is controlled by emotion. That is why you must have the place and conditions for your patients likely to induce in them a right emotional tone. The sick heart will not heal. The vitality is depressed by emotional states. It is reinforced by pleasurable ones, especially by interests and hope. And medicine is going to realise that it must count on secondary reactions as well as primary.

You should cultivate a method by which the vital forces can be freed by mental means from their inhibitions and distortions, and can be invoked by spiritual means and concentrated in the form and at the place where they are needed.

These methods do not apply to the entirely unevolved person, who in extreme cases might seem a more suitable subject for veterinary science, but they are of vital importance in dealing with those of a higher spiritual sensitivity. Orthodox

Principles of Esoteric Healing

science does not recognise the difference of type in its patients, but diseases kill or are cured differently in different types. It is the mental factor in disease and therapy that needs to be more closely studied.

Your patients will fall into two classes:

1. those in whom a deep seated emotional disturbance is affecting the bodily functions;

2. those in whom the physical condition is affecting the emotional states, which may be due to two minor causes:

   a) endocrine unbalance, or

   b) toxaemia in all its subtle aspects, which may have produced an emotional disturbance which in turn is depressing the bodily functions.

Diathesis

Study should be made of what is known as diathesis. That is to say a particular condition or habit of body or mind , especially one disposing to certain diseases.

Now what is it that predisposes? What makes a resistance low in one particular segment of the being? What causes a specific lowering of resistance rather than a general lowering? Why do some people have colds and not get other types of diseases?

You will have observed the temperament which shows itself when the disease has developed. What of it before it developed? Was it not latent in the reincarnating Ego? There, in a past life you have the origin of disease. Go back. That is where your diseased temperament originated. The disease does not cause the temperament; the temperament causes the disease — it comes out. Spots do not cause the fever.

Remember this, all the manifestations on the physical plane, even the so-called cure, are a symptom. Now you will understand why a straightforward surgical case shows no trace in

Therapeutic Methods

the disposition. A man's body may be shattered by an accident, but there is not change in his disposition.

When consciousness is disturbed at a certain level, it is those stuctures in the body which correspond in evolutionary development that will be disturbed.

If a case is liable to disturbance of bone tissue, another to disturbance of the organ of nutrition, it is because there is some disturbance in consciousness at the corresponding level, and the resistance of the corresponding stresses is low, and vitality reduced by conflict. Thus you account for what is called diathesis.

And that can be carried further. Why does a given person get a given disease? Why is one affected by infection of one type and one with another? Why is it one has bone disease and one disease of the organ of nutrition? Another, disease of the nerves? I will tell you. There will be a disturbance in that person in consciousness at the level corresponding to the particular aspect of the mechanism, and that disease reduces the vitality of the etheric double; it reduces its life, and then there is a weak spot in the aura and the ever present attack from outside comes in.

We correlate these things under the names of the planets, and you can correlate the planets again with the ten Holy Sephiroth, and you will find the different aspects refer to the different aspects of the celestial man. That gives you important keys. Excretion to the Earth. Reproduction to the Moon. Assimilation to the Sun. Co-ordination, or in other words brain and spine, to Daath.

Remember Daath is always on a different plane to the others. Daath is the apex of the triangle of which Kether, Chokmah and Binah are the three basal points. And Daath may be conceived as penetrating through to a corresponding point in the lower aspect of the Tree on the plane of Earth.

Principles of Esoteric Healing

People think that Kether connects with Malkuth of the higher, but that is not so, because that which emanates from Malkuth downwards is the averse Sephiroth of that Tree. And if you try to secure the reflection you get the averse aspect. But a very important secret is that you insert the apex of Daath into the Yesod of the Tree. You will see more in that as time goes on. You will see that if Daath is inserted into Yesod, then the Kether of the lower system appears in Tiphareth of the higher. These things require much thought.

The emotional brain is the solar plexus. You feel with your solar plexus. The brain itself correlates emotion and sensation. This takes place in the subtle body of the higher Tree, and the point of correlation between the higher and the lower is the pyramid of Daath.

The brain supplies the raw material for this. That is why impairment of the brain affects thought. Thought does not take place in the brain, but above and behind the brain, and emotion is in the solar plexus.

Have you ever tried, in talking to a person, to talk to the back of the head and not to the face? When you talk to the face you speak to the surface of the mind, but when you talk to the back of the head you talk to the subconscious mind. Think of that spot, concentrate on it. The face slides out of focus and you are talking to Daath, whether they realise it or not, the deeper self in the individual.

Suppose you have a difficult patient. You try to reason, and they resist. Talk to the base, just behind the head, and you will find you have touched the deeper self. That is the point to direct attention to. And learn to look at them with the third eye, situated in the triangle between the brows at the base of the nose.

And remember this, it is in that deeper self that lie the issues of life and death; there the subtle forces are directed. It

Therapeutic Methods

is useless to reason with the conscious mind without taking into account the deeper self, which has its own motives — which are Cosmic and evolutionary.

There are effects in biological time and different systems of bodily development, and there are corresponding epochs in periodic life waves, where corresponding phases of consciousness were developed. The key is in *The Cosmic Doctrine*. And it is upon the framework of the corresponding subtle phase that the dense wave evolves.

Primary and Secondary Reactions in relation to Treatment

I would give you counsel with regard to the use of drugs employed in the modern pharmacopoeia. Many of them being highly concentrated and presented in their most active form are too drastic in their actions. Remember that action and reaction are always equal and opposite, and the drug which is counteracting the manifestation of a disease has to use the constitution as a thrust block, and drug poisonings are much more subtle and far reaching than is sometimes suspected.

It is noteworthy that the person who never takes medicine never seems to need any, but the person who once starts on a course of drugging is always needing some fresh potion for some fresh symptoms. Fling a stone into a pool and the ripples spread to its circumference. Fling a potent drug into the metabolic system and the entire system has to effect adjustments.

Drastic methods are needed in acute conditions because the time element is a factor, but after you have had your patient on a course of drugs, take him off them on to a course of herbal remedies, thence, by way of the medicinal diets, back to normal. Thus you will prevent the drug reactions from setting up a vicious circle.

Principles of Esoteric Healing

It is a great mistake to give drugs in too active a form unless the need for such treatment is urgent and immediate. The whole tendency of medicine should be increasingly to get away from drastic interference from without, to regimes allowing and assisting nature to make the adjustments by natural means.

The vital point in all vital processes is vitality. I am not so much proposing to put before you a new system of medicine, as to bring you to a new attitude towards medicine. Your aim should not be so much to counteract symptoms, unless those symptoms be urgent, in which case you must perforce counteract them, as to co-operate with nature in her efforts to compensate a departure from the norm.

Always bear in mind that a departure from the norm is the point of origin in all disease, and the subsequent symptoms are partly a reaction and partly an attempt to compensate. Learn to discern between the reaction and the compensation. Assist the compensation, and compensate the reaction.

Beware always of drastic interference with nature. It invariably produces a reaction.

Now think what that means. You introduce into the human machine a powerful alterative. It changes the immediate conditions in particular reactions of the organism. That is the primary result.

But the human machine is a system of interacting units, and you cannot deal with any organ as an isolated unit. When you alter the condition of an organ, the whole organism has to readjust itself, and the secondary reactions are comprised in that readjustment. The reactions go cannoning through the organism, rebounding from one to another, to every unit in the human machine.

The pendulum has become inclined too far in the direction of inaction in a particular organ. You give it a violent push

Therapeutic Methods

towards action. Compensatory action is gone through, and is attended by reaction. So that if you call up activities throughout the organism you must be prepared for depletion, as a fire burns out under a gust; so you may stimulate one organ, and the consequences will be a depletion in another organ which has shared in the stimulus and burnt up its reserves.

Again, if you retard the action in the organ, be prepared for some remote function in the body to be clogged with effete matter. That is why you will often observe that people who start medicines for one disease, end with a perfect chemist's shop, dealing with reactions from the soles of the feet to the crown of the head. The more effectual the action, the more distinct the reaction.

The medicine of the future should use less the concentrated drug, and depend on a regime which works comparatively steadily and creates no reaction.

Learn the drug values of foods. In acute conditions you may be obliged to use drastic medicines because you have not time to work with the more gradual methods. But always remember the two reactions — the primary and the secondary. The secondary reaction must follow the primary reaction if balancing is to be achieved. Any drastic remedy sets up oscillation. It is that which you have to balance back to an even keel.

Therefore use rather the methods which assist vital processes. Study carefully the medicinal effect of diets. Do your drugging as far as possible in an organic form. Prefer the infusion to the alkaloid, and the infusion of the fresh herb to the dried herb.

Take full advantage of such therapeutic methods as massage, remedial exercises, electricity and radiant heat, and especially hydrotherapy. Homeopathy too is invaluable for highly

Principles of Esoteric Healing

evolved temperaments, to the young and the aged. In mental cases the effect of light and colour is very important indeed.

In dealing with your cases I would counsel you to have in the rooms they occupy a neutral sunlight background, and against that background have hangings of bright colour, changing the colour according to the requirements of temperament.

You must also remember that mental states are infectious, and mental disinfecting must be done after each case. Have as little in the rooms as possible; there is a serenity in emptiness. A nerve case should have as few objects as possible presented to consciousness; the mind should be kept still. Empty rooms and bright colour is your keynote.

To sum up then, you should use, on the physical plane, the more natural methods and the more diffused methods, rather than the more drastic methods.

Insomnia

In considering the subject of insomnia the principle is to treat the cause and also any secondary causes or symptoms so produced; these act and react one on the other. The general tone of physical health affects the sleeping, and if one is enabled to sleep more soundly, it will aid the physical recovery.

In a general way, if the physical body is in health, it is usually the emotional and mental factors that have a deleterious affect by inhibiting sleep. Insomnia, when of a chronic nature, produces a habit formation, which needs dealing with so that a proper habit of healthy sleep can be re-established.

Physical fatigue should be of assistance to sleep, but too much mental work is not beneficial. Work that tires the physical frame, rather than the brain, is the aim, in order to achieve

Therapeutic Methods

physical rather than mental fatigue, as it will draw down the forces from the mental level and help, in a natural manner, the desire to sleep. Therefore mental activity in the evening should be brought to a minimum in the early stages of treatment.

On general principles, the continued taking of any drug is very much contra-indicated in treatment unless it is absolutely essential. Drugs are of great value in helping the physical organism to make some adaptation, or to tide the physical body over some crisis. The use of sleeping tablets in cases of shock is undoubtedly a good thing. But if anything of that type, whether sleeping tablets, aperients, or indigestion aids, were to be taken as a permanent adjunct to assist the individual's metabolism, then it is not a good thing. It does not assist the organism to make its own adjustments to the situation towards a fully healthy functioning of whatever organ or function is concerned. The body has to make an adaptation to whatever medicine is taken and therefore there are repercussions in other aspects in one way or another. You must always remember that in the very deepest levels of the physical body there is a will to full healthy functioning; and the aim of healing should be to allow this to have a clear way.

On all ordinary occasions, attempt to dispense entirely with the use of opiates if the habit has been formed, unless of course any contingencies of a special medical nature might require them. With that proviso, this recommendation is made in the treatment of insomnia, mainly in order to shift the focus of reliance onto the inner physiological forces which will bring natural sleep. Learn to give them your trust, however difficult it is at first if past experience has shaken belief in the naturalness of the onset of normal sleep.

Try with perseverance to do this, and then instead of there being a vicious circle there will be another circle, but this time of better sleep bringing faith of a better nature in the ability to sleep. And this ability to sleep will build up the

Principles of Esoteric Healing

nervous system and quieten the mind. You must try to give nature a chance to allow the natural habit of going to sleep without medicaments.

In assisting sleep, relaxation is a very important factor. Physical relaxation is something that can be learnt and regularly practised. So also can mental relaxation, where the mind becomes passive. Particular types of music may be of benefit also.

There is no real danger to be feared from lack of sleep for a time. A fair trial should be given to dispensing with hypnotics for a time, in order to co-operate with that aspect of one's physical body on an almost vegetative level. This level has nothing to do with the concrete mind , which is a very much later development. If left to itself, by inducing a state of relaxation at all levels, it should be able to get on with its own job of proper functioning, of which sound and healthy sleep is one aspect. A long evening walk before retiring to bed is of help in bringing about physical rather than mental fatigue.

With prolonged lack of sleep, the etheric body becomes weakened, with a great liability for the etheric forces to leak away. This is more likely to occur in people of a sensitive constitution.

In these cases, it is evident that the line of treatment is to break the vicious circle at some point, because, naturally,the etheric depletion aggravates the insomnia, and the insomnia aggravates the etheric depletion. In these cases work on the personality level of the Tree of Life is indicated, with the circuit flowing upwards, so that the Earth forces may be built up and sustain the weakened etheric, so that it may, in its own turn, sustain the impact of forces from above. Stimulation of the higher Centres is harmful until the condition has righted itself.

In the diagnosis of these cases care should be taken to ensure that all the Sephiroth are in a healthy condition, for, due

Therapeutic Methods

to the etheric condition, rapports and diseased conditions may have become attached to them. If this is the case, special treatment will be required to clear up these Sephiroth. Once the etheric can be built up by means of assistance, increased sleep and therefore a better etheric condition will arise.

There are various ways in which the etheric Earth forces may be used in treatment. Meditation on the Earth forces under any acceptable symbol, before going to bed, or even in bed, will be of help. Remember the law of reversed effort, and avoid worrying as to whether you will sleep or not. By contacting the Earth forces, whether you sleep or not, they will have a strengthening effect on the etheric force, which is one of the main things that is derived from sleep. Some people can do with very little sleep when they are able to tap these forces at will.

As a meditation exercise preparatory to sleeping, the mountain journey to a Greek Temple of Healing can be taken. Imagine yourself lying down on a pastos awaiting the temple sleep which used to fall upon the patients awaiting healing there, and in that temple sleep the god or goddess would visit. This form of visualisation should be done with no sense of strain. In that Temple the goddess can be contacted, and she is very intimately connected with the Earth forces. She would be a helpful deity to meditate on in this connection whilst preparing for sleep.

If stronger Earth forces are required in the treatment of a generalised etheric weakening, you could use the forces of Asclepios Apollo, working upwards in combination with the soothing influence of the goddess. The Earth forces of Asclepios soothe and make healthy and whole all the Centres. Either he or the goddess can, however, do invididual work upon a particular Centre requiring attention. In order to work on all the Four Worlds of the etheric, you would use the god forms from each of the four quadrants in rotation.

Principles of Esoteric Healing

Meditation Sequence on the Temple of Asclepios-Apollo

The following pictorial meditation may be used as described above or as a preparation for any healing work on oneself or upon others. Coloured photographs of the region around the Greek temple complex of Epidaurus may also be of help as an aid to visualisation, or failing that of any typical Greek countryside. It may also be a help to have someone read it aloud or to record a tape of it. The reading should be slow and evocative, giving plenty of time for the images to build.

See yourself in the Golden Age of Greece in its splendour when there was that balance and harmony between the things of the body and of the mind, and when the healing gods and goddesses were worshipped.

Leave behind the serene calm of the Mediterranean and go forth as a pilgrim patient to the Temple of Asclepios-Apollo. Before long the pilgrim way leads upwards towards the mountain. The radiant sun shines down from the blue sky above. The winding path is thickly coated with white dust which eddies behind you as you climb in your sandalled feet. A mule walks beside you bearing your baggage and gifts for the temple. Only a few sparse bushes are seen on the short grass around.

Halfway up the mountain is a level plateau upon which the Temple stands. Passing through the outer entrance you enter the central courtyard, enclosed by the temple buildings. Around you there is a great deal of activity, and the priests and priestesses can be seen ministering to the sick and other pilgrims who are there before you. Leaving your mule, you go to the healing spring from whence you drink and ritually bathe in one of the stone basins connected thereto.

Therapeutic Methods

The temple lies opposite to the entrance and you now enter its sacred precincts, bearing your gifts with you. It is very cool and dim within. You can discern that the shape of the Temple is circular, and around you rise white marble pillars. The interior is austere and plain. The paving is of black and white and terra cotta, upon which aromatic herbs are strewn. In the centre is the altar with a rose light upon it. Before it, is the white marble pastos. In the East stands the statue to golden Apollo, and in the West, the statue to great Asclepios with his serpent-entwined staff. By his side and to the north is the statue to his daughter, the goddess Hygeia. Around the temple is a circular stone seat. You lay your gifts beside the altar and seat yourself in meditation.

See yourself in this Temple of Asclepios-Apollo. See the astral temple and feel its healing and sacred atmosphere. Meditate awhile now on the spiritual plane and open yourself to the healing and spiritual forces.

The Use of Consecrated Oil in treating Etheric Leakage

Consecrated oil is a form of useful treatment, because a film of oil prevents etheric leakage. The symbol of the goddess Hygieia is a lamp of baked clay filled with oil, and with the flame ever burning from its side. She bears this in her arms and the oil is olive oil, warm and scented.

The practice of anointing the dying with holy oil was to prevent obsession through the Centres, but you can learn the lesson and apply it in another way, so that the anointing with oil consecrated by the god Asclepios over the Centres should act as a barrier against impingement from without.

Regarding the ritual techniques of consecration, the bottle of oil stands upon the Tree in the centre. The name of Asclepios Apollo should be used, as you want the oil to have as general an application as may be; and in your invocation

Principles of Esoteric Healing

use also the name of the goddess Hygieia, as she too will add her measure of healing force, and direct her especial Elementals that function on the healing side of things. These healing Elementals are small units of elemental power that direct force. Many of them are like flecks of golden light, but they are living entities nevertheless.

Concerning the rationale of treatment, you are really making a talisman. The oil forms the focussing point for the forces in a similar fashion as ritual objects which are used as channels for forces in rituals. Therefore the bottle of oil should be covered and the same rules should apply as to other ritual objects, in order to maintain its etheric and astral counterparts unaltered.

Its use and application should be done under suitable ritual conditions. That is, such as you might do in a private meditation, first sealing and only having dim lights, and it should be covered up after use. A ritual bath should be taken beforehand, partly as a tribute to the goddess Hygieia, and partly as a symbolic action on all the planes.

In applying the oil, use the form of gesture that was common to Asclepios the god. In Greece the god Asclepios was often portrayed as laying his hands on the sick, and he did it in a particular manner. This is suggested, as it would link somewhat with the type of potency used, as if the God himself were anointing with the oil. To lie in bed on a white sheet, too, might form a symbolic representation of the pastos upon which the patient could lie during the night and be visited by the god.

Self administration is quite suitable, touching the seven Centres in turn, beginning with the Crown. None of the Centres exactly correspond with the physical, and the etheric and astral Centres of the Crown are above the head; you are making

Therapeutic Methods

a ritual act on the physical plane, and you touch the nearest physical approximation, which would be the crown of the head.

Concerning the duration of the potency of the oil when first applied, the same would apply as with sealing, because it is the etheric and astral portions that are potent, and they would last in a similar fashion to the astral effect of sealing generally.

This consecrated oil should be used when there is need for banishing your aura, for example, after any risk of rapport attachment. After the banishing, then apply the oil. It can also be used on occasions when you feel very mentally over-tired or over-strung, and might find difficulty in sleeping, as this will prevent a too drastic impingement of vibrations from outside on your Centres, but you should not make a habitual use of it. It may also be used before going to sleep if there is any danger of an actual astral attack.

The healing aspect of the oil mainly comes through your own organism, which contains its own power to heal within itself. All a doctor does with a patient really is to remove obstacles to natural healing. This oil does a similar thing on the subtler levels. You might say it acted as an astral disinfectant, and it would also prevent outside matter impinging on the Centres when not wanted, and your own subtle bodies could then go on unhindered with their own building up process.

Rapports: Obessession and Overshadowing — Origin and Treatment

Nothing from outside can obtain any power over the soul except by a rapport with that which is inside. There is always co-operation in obsession, and you must alter the conditions in the soul of that person, which caused him to enter into sympathetic relationship with the obsessing entity. Things may have gone much further than was intended, but there was an original response to the impulse, which opened the

Principles of Esoteric Healing

gate of the soul. The castle of the soul cannot be stormed, it is only betrayed by treachery.

A person is absolutely safe from any form of attack unless he is frightened, and then can be shocked into opening the gate; or unless the lower nature has a secret bond of affinity with that which attacks, and the entity which overshadows offers certain bribes to the garrison.

Two of the commonest bribes are the gratification of lust, and the gratification of hate or revenge. These two things, and sheer panic, are the things which open the gate to obsession; and the only way you will ever permanently cure an obsession is to cure the fear, the lust and the hate, for as fast as you close the gates they will open them again.

But you cannot undertake the cure of the case until you can lift the influence of the obsessing entity, and that you do temporarily by the force of your own will, taking care to protect yourself in the Name and Sign of the Master of Masters whom we all serve — Jesus the Christ. For an obsessing entity can turn on you, and then you have to guard yourself from the attack.

Therefore you cast the entity out, and get the patient to shut the gates and keep them shut. You cast the entity out by your own strength but you must give the patient his lesson to learn. Therefore re-education is half the battle in obsession cases.

Remember this, you can and should destroy thought forms, but you should not attempt to destroy an Elemental, for it is a soul seeking the light. You banish an Elemental, you do not attack it. You send it away where it should be. Never destroy an entity — banish it, for it has its own problems to work out.

However, true obsession is very rare. In most cases it is an overshadowing, or influencing, and you can recognise a true

Therapeutic Methods

obsession by one sign — the pupils of the eyes do not react normally to light.

As long as the pupils of the eyes remain normal, you are not dealing with an actual obsession. As soon as there are changes in the pupils there are changes in the soul, for the obsessing entity is never able to effect control of the eye. The pupils may be dilated or contracted, but as long as they are normal, it is overshadowing not obsession. But when they become abnormal it is obsession.

Do not be misled by changes in facial appearance; these will go with changes of mood. Watch the eyes.

You will also find another useful point for distinguishing a case of obsession — the patient does not eat when under the influence of the entity.

Change of character, even to the extent of alternating personalities, is no proof of obsession. Change in the eye and refusal of food are strong evidence when they go together.

Overshadowing, for all practical purposes, serves the same purpose as obsession, but strange as it may seem, the damage done to a soul by overshadowing is much greater than that which takes place in obsession. For this reason — in obsession the soul is pushed out and therefore is not influenced by the obsessing entity, so when it returns, it returns in its pristine state

But the physical vehicle may be badly damaged by the obsessing entity who is a bad tenant. You must always be careful in the case of an obsession that suicide does not occur on the eve of a cure, for the obsessing entity may elect to destroy the human whom it has to quit.

In overshadowing, suicides do not take place as a rule, unless the soul in desperation seeks to break up the point of

Principles of Esoteric Healing

contact for the obsessing entity, in order to protect those it loves.

The cases in which you look out for suicides are the cases in which one such is calling another over for purposes of its own. But in all cases the Name and Sign of the Master Jesus are the things that heal.

The patient who has delusions of persecution will have an atmosphere full of demons of the corresponding Qlippothic aspect, and as fast as you get rid of them he will pick them up again. But you can help him by periodically clearing his atmosphere so that he is not re-infected. Clear the atmosphere as a routine measure. Clear it magically with sword and torch and pentacles. Clear it, and seal it as a precaution.

In each new case listen to it as well as look at it. Listen mentally, and always be careful to clear your own atmosphere when finishing with each case.

Nightmare is a dangerous symptom. Do a special ritual after each case, for something may be picked up in the way of psychic infection.

Banish after each day's work with the pentagram. You may well invoke with the pentagram at the start of each day's round. Do the operation mentally. You will find it difficult to turn right round on the astral because of the "cord." Step over it, you will soon learn the trick. There is always that difficulty in the North until you are experienced.

Re-educate the mind as a matter of course because you cannot break a rapport by banishing only. You must change subconscious conditions. You cannot cure a case by psychology only, but you can clear up astral conditions by magic.

If conditions are absorbed from patients, either in psychoanalytical or healing work, and if the rapport is not terminated afterwards, the "picked up" conditions will remain in

Therapeutic Methods

the aura and may attach themselves to a corresponding Sephirah causing it to become diseased.

In these cases it is more usual, especially with ordinary ones and those on the right hand Path, that the condition would be picked up in the operator rather than in the place of working, if the operation was performed under ritual conditions. For the rapport would only be between the operator and patient, and there would not necessarily be anything in the place of working producing any particular attraction towards it. There are, maybe, certain cases where an infected atmosphere is left behind, but if it is with an initiate of the right hand Path with which you were dealing, it is not likely to be anything like that.

During psycho-analytical and healing work, the operator's aura should not be insulated during treatment, for it is not desirable. You purify and seal your aura afterwards.

In analytical work, no doubt, the rapport operates, particularly in some Centres, rather differently than in forms of magical workings for healing purposes. But in both cases there is a rapport for the duration of the work. Afterwards there should follow the purification of the priest's aura. This banishing of the aura afterwards is the important thing — you do not want to banish your Temple, but your own aura, because it is with your own aura that you have been working during the operation.

In this banishing you should work with one of the healing gods or goddesses on its dark or destructive side. As to which one you choose, that is largely an individual matter, as it should be one that fits in with the type of working that you do.

In the Healing Temple the priesthood use the appropriate Grecian gods or goddesses. According to his aspect Apollo can be the "far-darter" on his destroying side. Even the God Asclepios himself on occasion is used in this manner when he

Principles of Esoteric Healing

comes as the Celestial Surgeon. Then, with all these gods and goddesses of the healing pantheon, metaphorically speaking, you can apply the soothing poultice or lance the boil — it is a matter of how you are working, and one god or goddess can have these two sides.

If ritual is required for clearing the absorbed foreign matter, the forces of the god Asclepios should be used, as they are of a very purifying, hardening and astringent nature. They would be used working down the aura.

This operation should be followed by the administration by the god and goddess of the Earth forces up the aura in order to build up the strength of the etheric again. Otherwise, the operation being of a surgical nature, the etheric aura will remain very depleted. Earth force applied by the god in this direction can be of a soothing nature, making all the Centres healthy and whole.

Esoteric Hygiene and Anti-Sepsis

In the ordinary way of working examination of a patient is done by physical means. When you are working in esoteric medicine you also employ psychic means and must cultivate the power to make a psychic examination. In making a psychic examination you must learn to differentiate between the subtle bodies, and diagnose separately the etheric, the emotional, the mental and the spiritual status of your patient.

In order to operate in this way you have to establish a rapport, and that rapport produces a temporary sensitivity to all psychic influences. Therefore it must be conducted under protection in an aseptic atmosphere. What is true of surgery on the physical plane is true of surgery on any plane. The law of asepsis must be strictly enforced.

Infection may arise from a surgical incision or from a subtle plane rapport. Just as you must guard your patient from

Therapeutic Methods

infection, so must you also guard yourself from infection from the patient. Remember, all psychic cases are contagious. Where they form a rapport, they infect.

Before you proceed to examine a growth psychically, you would do well to dress yourself in imagination as if you were about to operate physically. Visualise yourself enveloped in spotless white, leaving only your hands and your eyes.

And immediately after you have examined your patient, take first one hand and then the other in your own hands and make the gesture you would make if your hands were covered with thick soap suds. Wipe them off and shake your finger tips. This prevents any magnetism remaining. You have to have your hands outside the psychic envelope, so close that contact after you have made it.

The eye always projects, therefore infection through the eye would only take place if you were dealing with a more highly trained occultist than yourself. If you have reason to believe that this is occurring, visualise cutting the contact with a sword.

In the ordinary way psychic infection takes place through the hand, but between patients and nurses it may take place from the solar plexus. In this case it will not be so much an infection as a draining.

If anyone has reason to believe that they are dealing with a vampire type case which thus drains, the best protection is to keep the feet together and clasp the hands — fingers interlaced — and hold them over the solar plexus. The exact spot to protect is above the pit of the stomach and just below the sternum. That is the spot to be covered, and the hands will just cover it, when folded.

Remember that many patients will reach out and take hold of you via the solar plexus Centre especially during a psychic examination. Never allow this, for it depletes you.

Principles of Esoteric Healing

The solar plexus is only used in polarisation, when there is an exchange of vitality, and that is a very necessary thing in this work. This is the only way in which it can be done safely. Being properly polarised on the solar plexus you can work freely from the pineal centre for your intuitive diagnosing.

There is an old saying in medicine "never make friends with your patients." It could perhaps be put better this way — in dealing with subtle cases — be a friend to your patients, but never let your patients be a friend to you, or you cannot deal with them impersonally.

It is a sound principle not to eat with your patients. There is a great deal in the communal meal. When you eat the communal meal you build a bond of brotherhood. So if you do not desire to form that bond, do not eat with a man; do not allow him to share your meal or share his.

In treating a patient you will not be secure against relapse until each of the subtle bodies in turn has been wakened to function and put in circuit. Emotion controlling the etheric, mind controlling the emotions, and the spiritual nature controlling the mind on the one side, and in touch with the Logos on the other side. That is to say, patients are not completely healed until they have been put in touch with the divine contacts.

Is the system beginning to come clear for you? Your aim is regeneration, not the patching up of symptoms. It is the making of the whole man new.

6.
THE CENTRES

The Centres are of great importance. As in the macrocosm, the Sephiroth of the Tree of Life are of vital importance in understanding the relationship between the cosmos and its parts, so in man, the microcosm, the Centres are the Microcosmic Sephiroth, and in them are clues of great significance when rightly understood.

As you have in the macrocosm the Four Worlds, so also in man in reference to the Centres are there Four Worlds or four levels on which they operate.

You must not only consider which relative Centre you are mainly concerned with in your patient, but also with which of the Four Worlds in that Centre you are dealing. As with the Tree of Life generally, you cannot consider one apart from the others, because it is the relationship which is of importance.

There are four main Centres, though many others have been ascribed. In the Eastern system they are given in greater detail, seven being the usual number that is given. In the Western system seven Centres are also used, and these correlate with the Central Pillar of the Tree of Life.

To place them all on this Pillar, two of the Centres, on either side of Tiphareth, correlate with the Paths joining Chesed to Geburah and Netzach to Hod. You have, therefore, in man, the microcosm, seven Centres correlating to the Tree.

1. The Root Centre in Malkuth;
2. the Pelvic Centre in Yesod;

Principles of Esoteric Healing

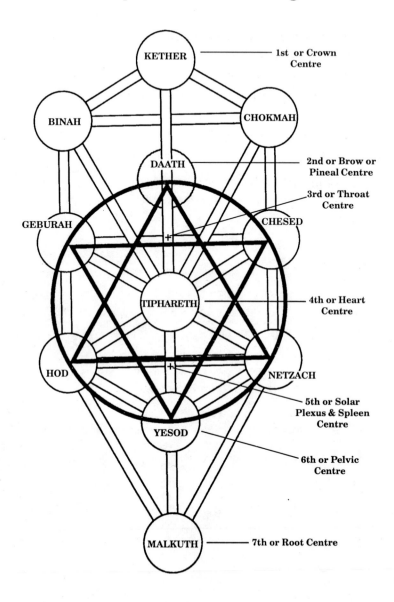

Tree of Life with Six Rayed Star or "Magical Circuit" and Etheric Centres

The Centres

3. the Splenic and Solar Plexus Centre at the intersection of Hod and Netzach with the Central Pillar;

4. the Heart Centre in Tiphareth;

5. the Throat Centre at the intersection of Chesed and Geburah with the Central Pillar;

6. the Pineal Centre in Daath;

7. the Crown Centre in Kether.

These are the seven Centres, and each of these is in the Four Worlds:

1. the etheric,

2. the emotional,

3. the mental,

4. the spiritual.

There is in Malkuth the physical World but it is the subtler aspects with which we are concerned. So when we speak of the Centres in Malkuth, it is really with the etheric or the subtler aspect of Malkuth or the Earth to which we are referring.

The Emotional level of the Centres is subdivided into that of the instincts and that of the higher emotions — or upper astral, as it is often called.

The Mental level is again subdivided into the concrete thinking principle, and the higher mind or intuitive level.

With the World of Spirit we have not much direct dealing, since there are no pathologies on that level, though it is with this level that we have to put the other levels in touch.

The Centres in the Four Worlds

In a condition of health, force should flow through the seven Centres from Malkuth upwards and also downwards from Kether, and the interplay of these two types of force

Principles of Esoteric Healing

manifests in the healthy functioning of the Centres. But when disorders arise you must not only consider which particular Centre is affected, which of course will show itself by the appropriate symptoms, but you must also diagnose whether the downward force or the upward one may be blocked partially.

There are three factors which play a part in the condition of health or otherwise of a Centre:

1. The actual state of the Centre itself. This is originally of karmic origin based on the etheric structure of the previous incarnation. It is, of course, modified for better or worse according to what is done in this life. This is the organ, so to speak — the subtle organ;
2. The quantity of force reaching out from Kether;
3. The quantity of force reaching out from Malkuth.

There is a physical plane analogy in the nervous system, whereby the actual nerve structure can be likened to a Centre, whether it is organically sound or not. Then the available nervous force would vary according to such factors as the general tone and the nutrition of the blood.

The astral plane is the meeting place for impulses arising from the plane below — that of the instincts — and for spiritual forces coming down from above. Both factors, if faulty, can lead to lack of balance on this plane, and the general principle can be applied more specifically when considering a particular Centre if you visualise the force flowing down or up.

In considering anything diagramatically, one must get back to the principle which it is intended to describe. The idea of the negative and positive forces which together work upon a Centre could be portrayed by visualising a Caduceus passing through each one. These negative and positive forces in the Caduceus form can either flow upwards or downwards, and in either case both principles act upon the Centre concerned. In normal functioning there should be an equal rhythm up

The Centres

and down, and alternating in the fashion of a caduceus through all the Centres.

Let us now consider the different Centres themselves, and those pathologies we might expect to find with their malfunctioning in the Four Worlds.

All these fourfold divisions into spirit, mind, emotion and body are only convenient classifications. The man is really a whole man, and if one Centre at a certain level — say the Emotional — is faulty, then the effects will work down to the World beneath in that same Centre. Although, of course, indirect repercussions will be felt in the other Centres.

1. The Crown Centre

The 1st Centre, of the Crown, correlates on the central Pillar with Kether and the influence of the whole Supernal Triangle.

a) In the first World, that of Spirit, there is nothing particular to say as there are no pathologies on that level, merely latencies if it is not fully functioning.

b) In the Mental World this Centre gives a faculty for grasping spiritual principles and archetypes.

c) In the Emotional World it gives a love for these things.

This Centre is only in a latent type of development or vivification in the once-born. Therefore from a practical point of view need not detain us.

2. The Brow Centre

The Brow Centre is situated on the Tree in Daath. This is a very important Centre particularly to those undergoing occult development.

117

Principles of Esoteric Healing

a) In the Spiritual World it is the means of contacting the Divine Spark of one's being in Kether. It is possible here to have a blockage between the Brow Centre and that of the Crown and when this occurs it is usually in a past life that the primary cause will have occurred.

b) On the Mental Level it is not usually very much awakened in the once-born, although c) is to a greater extent.

c) On the Emotional Level it is awakened to a greater extent in the once-born. In the twice-born b) and c) are usually operated together in magical work. It is the force in the Emotional World of Daath which is projected, but the formulating idea which directs that force is from the Mental World and inspired from the Spiritual World.

d) In the Material World the Brow Centre affects the endocrines which are correlated with it. These are the anterior and posterior pituitary and the pineal. Thus the Brow Centre on the physical level plays a major part in controlling the chemistry and therefore general functioning of the Personality as produced by its endocrine balance.

When you find a pathology on the Central Pillar at Daath or higher, it is probably always to past lives that you must look for primary causes. If it were something in this life, then you would find that that patient was perhaps in the process of taking some deviating step.

When there is constriction before Daath, the neurasthenic factor, that of hyper-sensitivity, would be an expected symptom, which, working down through the lower Worlds of Daath, would produce an effect upon the nervous system. If the resulting physical condition were one of insomnia and neurasthenia, one would recommend the Green Ray in all its aspects, that is to say all those factors of the Nature contacts which feed the second plane body of vitality. This would also include, partially in its sphere, the aspect of polarity.

118

The Centres

Occult or spiritual unbalanced development in past lives can result in either an over-development or under-development of a Centre in this life. The Daath Centre is the one used in magical work. It is rare to find a disturbance in this Centre in the under-developed — their trouble would be in the 6th or 4th Centres. But in cases where there has been occult development in the past in the 2nd Centre, and this was not fully balanced by the other Centres, it can produce a defective Brow Centre in this life, the resultant effects in a past life being carried by the Ghost and producing a defective Centre on the Etheric level in this life.

The general principles of treatment are to remove the primary cause and then to clear up the resultant symptoms. If the primary cause on the mental-emotional level has been removed, you then only have to clear up the results on the etheric level, and for this magic is a good method, by the direction and application of astral forces.

The Brow Centre is the seat of the intuitive sense and is of great importance in esoteric diagnosis. As in the development of all powers and functions you must visualise and concentrate upon them. In all development, the function, so to speak, precedes the organ, and is thus the reverse of what the more materialistic physiologists would aver. You can only learn to swim by trying to swim and believing in this ability, which, of course, is faith.

Where the Brow Centre is used for making an intuitive diagnosis, the Heart Centre is used for sensing a person's condition. Through the 4th Centre you can tell what is wrong, but not why it is wrong. Only in the 2nd Centre can you gain an understanding of the real causes of the disease.

This Centre is used when controlling lunatics or any person over whom it is desirable to exercise control for therapeutic reasons. It is also used for magically ridding patients of obsessions and, in fact, for any form of mental-magical healing. The powers of the Higher Self function through this Centre.

Principles of Esoteric Healing

3. *The Throat Centre*

The 3rd Centre, of the Throat, is situated on the Central Pillar at the intersection of Chesed and Geburah. Chesed and Geburah together form the anabolic and katabolic activities; they are also creative, and the Throat Centre is connected with creative activities — to some extent the 6th Centre on a higher arc. If you study the symbolism of the 19th Path joining Chesed and Geburah, further light will be thrown on that.

a) In the Spiritual World it is mostly concerned with creative activities.

b) In the Mental World it is again mainly concerned with creative activities but in a more concrete manner.

c) In the Emotional World it is partly concerned with the expression of the Personality and as much also of the Higher Self as is able to manifest through the Personality, and any frustration of the self-expression of a person as a Personality will give trouble in this Centre. It is not a specific aspect of self-expression of which we speak, as for instance that of the sexual would have repercussions on the 6th Centre, but of the expression of a person as a unique individual. They might have full sexual expression and yet be very frustrated people. In the Mental World also there would arise psychological difficulties connected therewith. It might arise in the Mental World first and then appear in the Emotional, or vice versa, depending on which was the primary cause.

d) In the Material World this etheric Centre will affect the physical endocrine glands correlated with it, that of the thyroid and thymus and parathyroid. There is rather an intimate connection between this Centre and the Pelvic Centre in Yesod; which shows also on the physical level by the antagonising action between the thyroid and the adrenals, which are correlated with the 6th Centre.

The Centres

4. The Heart Centre

The 4th Centre, of the Heart, is situated on the Central Pillar in Tiphareth.

a) In the Spiritual World there is no pathology but there could be a cutting off of the Centre from the ones above. The result would be a starvation as far as the force coming down from Kether was concerned, but not in those from Malkuth. In general terms it would be a Personality divorced wholly or partially from its Higher Self, and on the lower levels such a Personality may function in health, but that would only be in health as part of the whole man was concerned.

b) In the Mental World it is concerned with the perception of ideals.

c) On the Emotional level it is concerned with the feeling of unity, these are the particular astral emotions which function in this World and Centre.

d) In the Material World the Heart Centre has no correlation with the endocrine glands, but has with the nervous system, not the whole of the nervous system but part of it. There is also a correlation with the lymphatic system. This correspondence with the lymphatic circulation is mainly because some of the main lymphatic channels are situated, very roughly indeed, in this area. There is also some correlation when you consider the "four humours", which were taken very literally by many ancient time doctors, and the linkage with the physical temperament, so to speak, of the individual. Any of the four types may have correspondences here. Paracelsus spoke somewhat on the subject.

There could be here a pathology of either over-development or under-development in relation to the other Centres, and when this happens, too much or too little force is concentrated in them with a consequent upsetting of the equilibrium of the rest of the Tree.

Principles of Esoteric Healing

Let us consider the over-developed Heart Centre. Part of the cause of this is too great a concentration of force descending from Kether in relation to the ascending force from Malkuth. This condition is often found in those of a mystical temperament whose development has been one-sided. If there has been a lack of an equal up flow of force from Malkuth, it will usually be found that the Centres below the Heart Centre will be deficient in force, and therefore small.

The treatment mainly consists in concentration on those relatively undeveloped centres, (as that of the Heart Centre will already have had too much attention,) combined with an emphasis on the use of the Earth forces from Malkuth. These Earth forces can be applied in all Four Worlds. In the Material World it will be physical plane care and the use of Nature contacts to increase the physical vitality. The Emotional and Mental Worlds can be used — that is the Earth forces working through these Worlds — through visualisation by the patient himself or assisted by a healer. The spiritual essence of these Earth forces can also be applied by magical means.

Deficiencies in the Heart Centre usually manifest as psychological difficulties on the mental level, and it will also mean that the upper astral emotions are inadequate and undeveloped.

An excess of energy in this Centre can produce heart disease, due to excessive repercussions on the Centre which then affects the vagus nerve. Diseases of the sympathetic nervous system also might have a correlation. There is only too much energy in a Centre if it has no adequate outlet or if it is not balanced by other Centres. It is entirely a relative thing.

An excess of force, or an enlargement of the 4th Centre, is a cause of over-activity of the para-sympathetic system. A continuation of this after the Centre has returned to normal is due to habit tracks formed in the subtle side of the physical body which, even when the primary causative factor has been

The Centres

removed, may take a little while to settle down to normal. Also the physical effect of an illness leads to hyper-sensitivity generally and this would be especially noticeable in the weakest link.

The practice of autosuggestion can be used to train the autonomic mind which directs the running of the physical body, and is itself almost physical, into its new habits. The visualisation of the Tree and then the visualisation of the Centres and the currents between as they ought to be, is a symbolic way of obtaining the right type of relationship in the Mental Body.

Also visualisation, will and autosuggestion on a more physical level should be used. In a general way it is necessary to have a normal healthy functioning of the whole of the physical organism in order to counteract this habit track, and to allow the intelligence which directs the running of the physical body a free hand. This will take place at a very deep level of the subconscious, for it was developed very early in evolutionary time.

Twelve Petals are assigned to the Heart Centre. Generally speaking in ascending the microcosmic Central Pillar there is an increasing complexity in them, because they fulfil more and varied functions the higher they go. The number twelve has correspondence with the functions of the Heart Centre; perhaps capacities rather than functions would be a better word.

In the Root Centre there is a four-fold division, as it is concerned only with the Four Elements. In the Material World everything can be resolved to one of the Four Elements but in the higher Centres there is almost a geometrical progression in the increase of complexity and function. It is difficult for those living on the physical plane to comprehend this. This does not mean to say, of course, that there is not an underlying unity as well, but it is as if a three dimensional creature was trying to understand a four dimensional world.

Principles of Esoteric Healing

5. The Solar Plexus & Spleen Centre

The Solar Plexus is concerned with the nerve supply on a very low subconscious level, and the Spleen also with the nerve supply and esoterically with the intake of vitality. These are both functions belonging to the lower levels of the Personality, and therefore, on the Tree, they must go between Yesod and Tiphareth. Since we are putting them all on the Central Pillar, we may place them at the intersection of the transverse 27th Path, between Hod and Netzach. The Spleen and Solar Plexus Centres have fairly similar functions, and can be considered together from a practical point of view in making these correlations.

a) In the Spiritual World they are concerned with the dynamic energy of the individual. It is not so much a Centre that gives forth dynamic energy as do some of the others, it is rather a receiver and distributor of it.

b) On the Mental level it is concerned chiefly with assimilation of ideas.

c) On the Emotional level it is concerned with the reception of emotional impressions from the astral plane around. It is also a linking point for the emotions of the individual as they work down and affect the etheric centre in the World below, then expressed in physical consciousness.

d) On the Etheric level this Centre receives the etheric forces and distributes them over the rest of the microcosmic Tree. Earth magnetism passes up from the Root Centre in Malkuth, and it is from the Solar Plexus-Spleen Centre at the intersection of Hod and Netzach that it is distributed round the Tree.

The Etheric force goes to all parts of the auric Tree, but from one point of view, this Centre can be considered as being principally to do with the Personality. In this sense, it is more of a distributing Centre, when considering the individual, than

The Centres

the Heart Centre above, in Tiphareth, which is chiefly concerned with another type of force.

In a sense, the Solar Plexus & Spleen Centre is the distributing Centre for Etheric force from Malkuth, while that of Tiphareth, the Heart Centre, mediates the Spiritual force from Kether to all parts of the Tree. They are both mediators of forces, but of different kinds.

It is the Earth forces or magnetism which go to the 5th Centre, and these will contain the forces of the Four Elements, that of Fire amongst them. The forces of the physical Sun, therefore, come with the Earth magnetism.

It is that of the Spiritual Sun of Kether that comes down and is distributed through the 4th Centre. The intake of the Earth forces through this 5th Centre can be controlled by respiration if combined with the visual imagination.

Pathologies of the 5th Centre can be classified according to the Four Worlds.

a] On the Etheric level.

Generally speaking there will be either congestion or deficiency of force on the Etheric level of this Centre. Either of these conditions will eventually show in the dense physical body, that is, assuming a condition which has not primarily started in the physical.

With a congestive condition of force, there is likely to be endocrine disfunction and unbalance in the ductless glands associated with this Centre, the adrenals and pancreas, and there will be correlation also with the digestion and assimilation.

Similar physical symptoms may also be produced sometimes by the etheric conditions arising on other planes or by a deficiency of force in this Centre. That is just one added reason

Principles of Esoteric Healing

why you must always treat the cause of things and not only the symptoms.

The causes of the conditions just described on this level of the Solar Plexus & Spleen Centre may originate on the Etheric level itself, or on the levels above.

If the causes originate on the Etheric level, it is likely that they are due to:

i) general depletion of Etheric force due to greater expenditure of energy than there is intake — the output is not balanced by the inflow. Obvious examples are overwork and strain, with too little sleep, and so on. This type of condition is already well known to the medical profession, and there are quite common sense ways of dealing with them.

ii) the Centre itself is not normally formed and functioning, and this may be due to:

a) conditions originating from the past through the Ghost;

b) some condition such as shock or strain which has led to it;

c) conditions sometimes found in certain types of people who are very liable to leak Etheric force, which takes place mainly through this Centre. There are people with whom this leakage may happen automatically because of a faulty Centre;

d) in somewhat rarer cases, deliberate vampirism, which is dealt with in our section on Rapports.

b] On the Emotional level.

In causes originating above the Etheric level in practice there will usually be found factors on the Emotional level which will also affect the Etheric, even when there are also factors on the Etheric level itself which produce that condition.

The Centres

Emotional difficulties have a very great effect on the Etheric, and these can be subdivided into two types:
i) those arising out of non-fulfilment of the instincts, which is likely to lead to congestive conditions on the Etheric level, due to the damming up of force;
ii) emotional difficulties arising from psychological causes, and very generally speaking, this type of difficulty is likely to lead to a deficiency of force.

But nothing in man is really clear cut and to be considered by itself alone. An emotional difficulty arising from lack of instinctual satisfaction can give rise in time to psychological difficulties. And psychological difficulty can produce a lack of instinctual satisfaction, which will then give rise to emotional difficulties, because all these levels act one with another.

c] On the Mental level.

Trouble in the Etheric may have originated higher than the Emotional, that is, in the Mental World itself. Here you must remember that this Centre is at the intersection of Hod and Netzach, and on the Mental level this Centre is concerned with assimilation. It should be in contact with the macrocosmic Centres of Hod and Netzach which unite at this point. Thus it serves to carry out the energising drive of the instincts and emotions of Netzach. When there is pathology here, it will tend to manifest as a lack of proper co-ordination between the person and his environment on this level; in a sense he will fail to get to grips with his practical environment.

This Mental level is not concerned with intuition and things of the spirit as is the Centre of Daath on the Mental level, but it is concerned with adaptation to a person's environment, the assimilation and utilisation of aspects of the outside world which impinge upon that person and give him experience.

Principles of Esoteric Healing

d] On the Spiritual level.

Of the Spiritual level there is not much to say by way of inherent pathologies but there could be a lack of receptivity.

6. *The Pelvic Centre*

The Pelvic Centre is situated in the Sephirah Yesod on the Central Pillar of the microcosmic Tree. This Centre is the seat of Kundalini, around which so much controversy has taken place by many writers. It is mainly concerned with creative activity in all the Four Worlds.

a) In the Spiritual World it is dynamic.

b & c) In the Mental World it is rather linked with the instincts. This is the concrete mind rather than the intuitional, the mental function being concerned with the carrying into effect of the emotions and instincts of the Emotional World connected with this Centre. It is chiefly the instincts which promote the mentation here.

d) On the Etheric level it is the vehicle of the personal magnetism or physical dynamism of the individual.

This is a very important Centre, and there has been much teaching on some of its metaphysical implications which we need not deal with here, but we will consider more fully the pathologies that the Centre is subject to, which are many and complicated.

There is the Centre in the Four Worlds, and we also have to consider particularly the influences of the Centre of Malkuth below it, as well as the Centres above, as their actions have a very strong repercussing effect in the Pelvic Centre if there are pathologies elsewhere.

The Centres

a)The Material World.

With pathologies on this level the effects will be mainly some disfunction in the sexual sphere, as the gonads correlate with the 6th Centre. With this, there might be an upset in the vitality of the individual, but not necessarily so, as it would depend on why there was a disfunction on this level. As always, when anything is amiss in the Material World the procedure is first to exclude any physical plane causation. If it is present, then treat it, but also look further to see whether there are any antecedent causes in the planes above.

b)The Emotional World and c) the Mental World.

If there is a cause of trouble on the Emotional plane it is very likely that the instincts are not having normal expression. This again is not likely to be the first cause of such a condition, and then it is to the Mental level that you must look, for psychological factors that might produce a faulty or perverted attitude to the functions of this Centre. This is considering the Centre at the moment rather as an isolated unit, which of course, it is not in reality.

Another set of influences which all have a bearing and effect on this Centre are:

i) the influences from Malkuth — the Root Centre,

ii) those transmitted from the higher Centres on the Tree, as their influence would have to come down to the 6th Centre before coming through to the physical.

Let us consider first the influences from Malkuth. One possible source of a pathological condition is if there is any break in the flow of force from Malkuth to Yesod, of the Earth forces which should flow up. If there is such a break or blockage, there will be a condition of congestion and stagnation in the

Principles of Esoteric Healing

6th Centre. The results are likely to be mainly felt in the 7th Centre, so we will consider that further when we are considering the pathologies of the Root Centre.

Considering the influences from the other Centres above, which are likely to produce the Pelvic pathologies, there is a connection, in a sense, between the 6th Centre and the 2nd Centre in Daath.

Digressing for a moment, in the varying and complicated picture of the microcosmic man, bear in mind these polarising pairs of Centres:

The 1st polarises with the 7th

The 2nd polarises with the 6th

The 3rd polarises with the 5th

The 4th, Tiphareth, the Heart Centre, is the centre of the whole man himself.

Therefore, with a pathology in the Pelvic Centre, always examine the Brow Centre, as it is quite likely that that may be a determining factor in producing the pathological Pelvic one. Any perversions in the use of the 2nd Centre will have repercussions on the 6th Centre and render it liable to get a little out-of-hand, as these are Centres particularly of the use of force.

Perversions in this sense mean using the Centre contrary to the proper functioning of such a Centre when working for the Higher Self. All these Centres should be used under the guidance of the conductor of the orchestra, and if some do not listen, but try to play a tune by themselves, then that is perverting their true function.

Concerning the influences coming from the higher Sephiroth down to the Pelvic, if there is a lack of proper balance between any of the Sephiroth, then the Yesodic one is likely to be affected, as overbalance in one Centre is likely to lead to under-development in another.

The Centres

There are two other factors which produce pathologies in this Centre. One is the use of "spells", that is, a pathology produced by occult means; and the other the influence of Rapports.

The first can be considered on their own. The occult pathologies are quite an interesting subject, but not likely to be met with in the secular modern world. If a "spell" is laid upon a Centre, the 6th is very likely to be the one to which it would happen.

The reason is that it is the 6th Centre wherein resides Kundalini, the source of magical power in the individual. Although power can be raised by the individual to the other Centres, this Centre is the starting point for it. In the placing of a "spell" it is in this 6th Centre that there is likely to be a reaction between the individual and the other agent. It can be the point of entry for outside forces in the hypothetical case under consideration, and these are inimical forces. That is the explanation why such a Centre may be affected rather than another

The influence of Rapports on this Centre are not of such permanence, and do not cause such a great influence as those on the 5th and 4th Centres. Rapports on the Pelvic level are of short duration, and there is not that more or less permanent type of rapport as between the more emotional levels, which can go on all the time. But while a rapport is in operation, the question could arise of etheric sepsis if there is anything pathological in one of the Centres in question. With this Centre there is more risk of etheric sepsis than with other Centres. This is for the same reasons given concerning occultly produced pathology in the 6th Centre — it is a way of ingress for the forces.

The powers of this Centre, more than others, are the ones inclined to get disordered. They are mixed up with the fluidic Lunar currents, with emotions, and sometimes with lack of mental stability. The Moon is very fluidic, that is to say, very

Principles of Esoteric Healing

changeable, very sensitive. Therefore a Centre dealing with these things would be very likely to get out of order.

In patients it may be necessary to get the current flowing properly through from Kether, without any blockage. Or it may be that this Centre cannot contact the Root Centre properly. In the latter case there will be a lack of proper growth of the Personality all round. These people cannot find their way about in the world, or know what to do between Yesod and Malkuth. Until that blockage is removed they will not act properly.

Many kinds of things bring that blockage into action. Childhood has also to do with this Centre, especially wrongly treated childhood, for that will come under the Moon and upset this Centre a great deal. Treatment consists in setting the force moving down all the planes, and every endeavour should be made to remove any blockages if present, so long as the primary causes have been dealt with.

When the blockage has been removed, the direct results will come about fairly gradually. It depends on the age of the person as well as the nature and size of the blockage as to whether it is important or not. Whether it was through some foolish childhood experience of some sort, which may have created almost a mental condition, or whether it was something very much graver which has thoroughly upset the nature. Such things cannot be moved at once but where the person is willing and esoteric treatment is undertaken, and common sense and guidance also used, then that person should become wholly healed.

7. The Root Centre

The 7th Centre, the Root Centre, is situated on the Central Pillar in Malkuth. This Centre forms the link between the microcosmic Malkuth in man and the macrocosmic Malkuth from whence he derives his basic energy — from the Earth

The Centres

forces that flow up and energise the Personality. That is its function, and it is so on all the Four Worlds of Malkuth, for man requires energy from all the Four Elements.

Pathologies of the Root Centre in the Material World or the Etheric level are likely to manifest as a deficiency of force, and that of course can produce divergent ailments on the physical plane. The reasons for this deficiency of force may be due to physical causes, to overstrain and so on, or a lack of Earth forces coming up to this Centre.

The causes of the latter are likely to be on the Emotional and Mental levels. Factors on these levels producing a lack of the Earth forces in the Etheric World would manifest probably in a wrong attitude, such as an ascetic outlook, or too great an emphasis on the spiritual to the exclusion of the natural. The psychological factor would tend to produce the cutting off of the man from his roots, and his physical dynamism would suffer as a result.

There might also be a blockage somewhere in the Tree above Malkuth, and that again would prevent the force flowing freely down. The force is a two way circuit and if it cannot flow freely down, neither can it flow freely up, and so the individual will suffer.

Generally, as with the 6th Centre, pathologies in Malkuth such as under-development and so on are likely to be a result of all the influences come down the Tree from Kether. Any distortion in the forces of any of the Centres above will reflect down to Malkuth. In all these things there is the effect of action and reaction, and anything which is amiss with the Root Centre will also affect the other Centres.

The Root Centre is a very important one indeed, and in the fully developed individual the Centre of Malkuth should balance and polarise with the Crown Centre. It is between these two Centres that the currents from Heaven to Earth and Earth

Principles of Esoteric Healing

to Heaven flow, and the aim in all your healing work is to free the channels so that this may happen unimpeded.

The Centres in Diagnosis

The Centres form the gateways whereby man, the microcosm, touches the macrocosm. And also whereby the influences of man's subtler bodies permeate down to his brain consciousness. The Centres function in all Four Worlds and in any derangement of a Centre you must consider in which World it occurs.

First, make your diagnosis, finding first the primary cause, in what Centre and in what World or level. Then find what resultant symptoms have been produced by that primary cause, and on what levels or Centres these may now be operating.

This diagnosis cannot always be done quite in that order; sometimes you will start with the prime cause and follow it down — sometimes you will be faced with physical symptoms and you then trace them up. But a complete diagnosis must be made. Without that you are working in the dark, and might do more harm than good.

To make this diagnosis you use all the means and methods that you can have at your disposal. First the skill and knowledge of the medical profession, either of yourself or in consultation. In those complaints which may have physical origins you want to exclude those factors.

Then make what use you can also of clairvoyant diagnosis. You must have the case history of the patient on all levels, if possible, as that gives you pointers in the direction to look. A physician on the physical plane expects to have some case history from his patient; so must you also when dealing with soul conditions.

The Centres

Finally, with your intuitive powers, you must make a synthesis from all the knowledge that you have obtained by the foregoing means, and make your diagnosis. Of course it may not always be complete, or even completely accurate; such is not always the case with a physical diagnosis on the physical plane. But at any rate it gives you a working hypothesis when it comes to treatment; and, as in any physical plane treatment, you make the best diagnosis you can and you prescribe the best treatment you can, and you see what happens.

You should be very systematic in making a diagnosis and follow the same thorough lines as taught in clinical medicine. If you are unsystematic and uncertain of the complete diagnosis, you will also be in doubt of the correct treatment. Do your diagnosis systematically on the four levels.

Upon the purely physical level find out if there is anything wrong. Then the etheric. Then find out if there are any difficulties on the emotional plane. Lastly, find out the degree of harmony between the Lower Self and its Higher Self, its source of power and vitality. That is, considering the personality as a whole.

Then there is the matter of the case history. It will probably have to be brief. It would take too long to do in great detail. What factors in this life, such as childhood experiences, could have produced present psychological or emotional difficulties? If the factors in this life seem insufficient for what you find, then look back further to past lives. Try to get a complete picture of your patient — the personality in this life, its degree of union with its Higher Self, and the influences of the past which are operative upon it.

When you have obtained all these component parts, try to form a synthesis and make your diagnosis, and then treat to the best of your ability. When you have done this, you can do no more. It is better to attempt something rather than

Principles of Esoteric Healing

nothing. Even on the physical plane a doctor cannot always be one hundred percent sure of his diagnosis.

Intuitive diagnosis is partly dependent on observation of subtle factors, in the same way as a doctor looking at a patient has such a developed sense of observation, through much experience, that minute points will strike him and, often without consciously knowing why, he will give the right diagnosis. In the same way, remember that observation aids intuitive diagnosis. Intuition is knowledge that is not obtained through conscious reasoning. It is often almost subconscious observation which gives a basis for intuition to work upon. From a medical point of view you could to some extent define it as a hyper-development of intelligent observation.

With ordinary cases, follow the usual procedure of taking an esoteric case history, making any diagnosis you can, and using any information you can. It is possible for anyone to develop the ability to read the akashic records with perseverance, but here the principle of the economy of effort and of your time comes in. It might be more economical to specialise in other things and have someone to do this for you. But you might well develop an intuitive sense regarding the past lives of a patient which, while not giving any precise details, would yet give enough of a general impression of the factors producing a given condition to enable you to decide how to treat it.

Of course sometimes there might be cases of an acute nature in which the need was so urgent that you give useful treatment without knowing all the facts. Always some such cases arise, but they are equivalent to emergency operations on the physical plane. In ordinary cases you must endeavour to be systematic and not to jump stages.

To diagnose the particular World which is at fault for any given Centre you must diagnose by the symptoms. This unbalance may arise from the level above that of the physical,

The Centres

or from the emotional or psychological; that is but another way of saying the Emotional World or the Mental World and in any one of these levels the origin may be found. In these Worlds you will have the corresponding Centre to whatever physical condition is being discerned.

Often the first three worlds are all interconnected. In such a disease the Centre is affected on all these three Worlds or levels because, for example, if the mental or emotional level of a Centre is disturbed for any length of time, the disturbance will work down to the physical and in due course some disease will appear.

Equally, some diseases which may have originated on the physical plane or perhaps that next to it by depletion of vitality due to strain or overwork, or lack of obeying the rules of hygiene, will affect the emotional level if the resulting disease produced by these factors continues. It will have a depressant effect upon the emotional level and so it will work up. That is why I always stress that you must deal with a disease at the point where the disharmony first occurred, then follow up or down as the case may be, and clear up the secondary and following symptoms which are produced.

Under-activity or over-activity of a Centre is diagnosed by the intuitive or clairvoyant method. A partly functioning Centre will not appear so bright, but this does not necessarily indicate actual physical disease unless that condition had reached down the planes. Conversely, if physical disease is present originating on the physical plane, for example blood poisoning, the effect on consciousness, working upward through the endocrines and the etheric, will in its turn affect those Centres and impair full functioning, because the flow of vitality will be affected.

The colours vary according to the Centres concerned, as upon the Tree, but it is their intensity which indicates their state.

Principles of Esoteric Healing

When there is under-activity it will be seen that something is wrong, or will be wrong upon the physical plane. Yet over-activity will only cause unbalance if it is not compensated by a similar development in the others. It is here a question of balance.

It may be seen that there is individual variation in the development of the Sephiroth in the aura. This is partly a question of potential and according to which Sephirah attention is habitually focussed and made use of. When the emphasis is on a particular Sephirah, it will develop, but not necessarily equally in the Four Worlds, as it would not necessarily be used in all its aspects.

You would thus get development of a Centre but not equal development. A Centre could also be well-balanced and yet on a low potential and therefore appear small. One could have in theory a Tree completely balanced in all its Sephiroth, yet on a low potential, and another Tree on a high potential. There are innumerable permutations between these two possibilities. Growth is very unlikely to take place equally in all the Sephiroth and therefore temporary unbalance will occur.

When certain figures build up in the Centres they represent Potencies and are symbols. You cannot, or a psychic cannot, see a Potency direct very well, so a symbol is seen that represents that Potency. If a certain figure were seen in Tiphareth it might indicate that a certain potency was present in one of the Four Worlds of Tiphareth, the World to which in symbolism that figure would correspond.

In differentiating between the Four Worlds in a Sephirah the colours are one distinction; also the symbols that build up usually symbolise one of the Four Worlds. For instance, if you saw a Child, or a crowned King or the Crucified One in Tiphareth, it would not be hard to decide to which world it referred.

138

The Centres

Actually, different psychics may see different symbols, but that which is symbolised, if the reading is correct, would be the same. It is really the psychic who can more easily interpret her own symbols because she usually knows to what they correspond, although of course there is a general convention of Mystery symbolism, with which you should be familiar.

The symbolism would indicate the condition. This condition might be normal or it might be ailing, but the treatment will depend upon the diagnosis which is made after finding out the condition of the patient. In healing we try to understand as fully as possible what precisely is wrong, and why, before we treat it.

Overdevelopment of the Sephirah Hod, for example, when not compensated, leads to separateness producing the effect of an undue focussing in the Personality. That is, an overdevelopment of aspects of the concrete mind, rather than the intuitive — which appertains to the Tiphareth level.

If a rigidity is seen in the upper Sephiroth of a person's Tree during an auric reading, it can be due to a partial separation from the Higher Self in the past. The result is a spiritual stiffness through disuse of a vital link. As an analogy, like muscle tissue which when disused produces stiffness and atrophy.

Should there be an uneven blockage in the forces on the Central Pillar, observation directed to the Side Pillars will often throw light upon it. If the blockage is on the left part of the Central channel, note also that the left Pillar is the Pillar of Mercy — also the Pillar of Force — and that it is also on that side Pillar that the Green Ray in many of its attributes is placed.

The influence of the Side Pillars — even when there is no specific deficiency or overplus — is felt in the Central Pillar, for it is the Pairs of Opposites in the Side Pillars which are

Principles of Esoteric Healing

resolved in the Central Sephiroth, and if there is unbalance in the Side Pillars, the effect in consciousness will be an unbalance in the Central Sephiroth. When the blockage is on the left part of the Central channel, the Green Ray, which also includes the dynamic Power aspect, would be of benefit, because it is partly on that left Pillar that you must work to equilibrate that side of the Central Pillar.

General Principles of Treatment in the Four Worlds

Having made your diagnosis, you come to the question of treatment. This will vary according to the Centre concerned, and to the level on which that Centre is malfunctioning. Let us consider the varying disabilities and how, in general principle, you would treat each type.

The Spiritual World or World of Atziluth

You would not have trouble in any of the Centres on the Spiritual Plane, because there is no disharmony there, but there may be a break between that Centre and the one below. That could happen, but we cannot go more deeply into it now.

The Mental World or World of Briah

Any of the seven Centres could be faulty on the Mental level. Here you are in the realm of mind, of psychology and planetary forces, for the planets have a correlation with the psychological states in man. Their influence is first through men's minds. This does not work directly down to the physical, but only as mental states influence psychological reactions.

You can get the same effect as the ancients used to obtain by focussing a particular planetary influence upon a patient,

The Centres

by concentrating upon the particular Sephirah with which it correlates in the aura of the patient, in his microcosmic Tree.

This has to be used with great understanding, as those of the side Pillars by themselves are unbalanced. You must have discrimination to know which Sephirah needs balancing, because with a lack of balance on one side you may not have looked far back enough and seen where this unbalance originated. Matters are not at all simple.

For instance, supposing there is a relative deficiency in Netzach, you cannot simply say Hod has too much and must be compensated by more Netzach. You must consider the Paths upon the Tree and, in this case, both an over-developed Hod or an under-developed Yesod would result in inadequacy in Netzach. Also there is the link between Netzach and Mars, and an inadequacy in Geburah tends also to have an inadequacy in Netzach.

The ancients tended very much to exteriorise everything, to project, and that was why so much was made in those days of stellar magic and its potencies. Now the emphasis has rather changed, and man is beginning to realise that all the forces are in his own nature, and so he does not have to think of this or that planet outside, as it is all within.

With these planetary influences beware attempting them with patients unless you have a very clear diagnosis, as they are unbalanced forces when on the side Pillars. You can, of course, try them on yourself if you will, as you will probably have a better idea of your own make-up than of another's. With experience, however, it can be a very valuable therapeutic method.

This mental level is a very wide field and cannot be covered adequately in passing other than to indicate that there is considerable scope for further amplification and correlation — how the different psychological states, through pathologies,

Principles of Esoteric Healing

produce malfunctioning of the Centres that correspond to particular complexes and faulty aspects within the psyche.

The Emotional or Astral World or World of Yetzirah

Turning to the seven Centres on the emotional level we are concerned mainly with two aspects.

1. Trouble arising on this level through faulty adjustments with the Instinctive plane, with frustrations or inadequate expression, or even over-indulgence. These can all produce disturbance of the emotional Centres. To some extent the Centre concerned would vary according to which instinct, or which combination of instincts, was giving trouble. You have three instincts usually known as the self-preservation instinct, the reproductive instinct, and the herd instinct. The image making faculty of the mind is an organ, not an instinct. An instinct is a force, the image making faculty of the mind is a mechanism.

2. Disturbance of the emotional Centres produced by a faulty condition between the emotions of the person and the realm of the Spirit. The person may be maladjusted to God — not in tune with the evolutionary forces, or his own Essential Self or Divine Spark. If he is out of tune here, however much instinctual satisfaction he may be having, he will still have trouble on the emotional level and disturbance of the emotional Centre.

So there are these two directions in which to look. For treatment, of course, you must endeavour to put right that which is producing the trouble. This you can only do by helping the patient to do it himself.

If it has arisen from a spiritual disharmony you help the patient to adjust himself to that Divine Centre of his own being. But you can only help the person who wants to be helped, who feels in need of help, and who is prepared to face the truth concerning his condition, otherwise he will blame all else but the truth and you cannot help him.

The Centres

This raises another point that you must bear in mind when taking a case history from any patient. You must assume no co-operation when eliciting facts, and do not expect them to be forthcoming. If they are, so much the better. You must frame your questions so that they range in broad sweeps over possibilities. Your patients may only answer what they are asked and no more, or they may not realise the significance of what they withold. Mental realisations are a thing of slow growth. You cannot push a person beyond their spiritual realisations; you can only assist in the process.

You can sometimes help those whose difficulties arise through frustrations or over-indulgence of the instincts, by assisting them to understand themselves and their instincts, and to make their difficulties conscious, so that they can come to terms with them and perhaps find a solution for themselves.

With the instincts, it is when the frustrations and repressions are in the subconscious that the greatest damage is produced. When a situation concerning the instincts is conscious, the patient can perhaps find some way of expressing them, or diverting them into other channels. Or, if their indulgence would cut across other factors which they hold dearer, then, perhaps, they could make a conscious sacrifice and gain power thereby.

The Physical/Etheric World or Material World or World of Assiah

We come now to the seven Centres on the plane of Malkuth — the subtler level of Malkuth — and it is here that the sphere of magic and magical methods of treatment are mainly concerned, for it can be moulded by the astral forces which are directed by the mind.

You can direct the forces where you will on this level, but it should only be done when you know what you are doing and why. This is because, unless you have cleared up the primary

Principles of Esoteric Healing

factors, they will only recur and cause greater unbalance by repercussions on other Centres and levels. But if you have dealt with the primary factors first, then treatment by magical means on this level can have very speedy results, because of the amenability of this level.

It is here that the forces of Asclepios-Apollo have a very potent influence, and you want to learn to direct them intelligently. For you, as priests of medicine, in a sense become and represent more and more that god himself when you are in your healing function. And as him, you must learn to direct these forces. And how can you direct these forces until you know into which direction they are to be directed?

This is the sphere pre-eminently of many traditional methods of treatment in the past, which the medical profession are finding efficacious but do not know why. The reason is that these methods affect the etheric level of the Centres, and it is on this level that you have the direct link with the endocrine system, and the endocrines link with the consciousness and personality make-up of the patient.

You are here working directly on to the physical plane from the plane above. The rule is that you always operate on a plane with the same forces as that plane, but directed from the plane above. There is always an unbroken chain between spirit and matter, but it is the plane above working down, or the plane below working up, that immediately affects the plane in question. Therefore in treatment you always have to consider this factor.

In any derangement of a Centre you must consider in which World it occurs. In the Material World, which is fringing on to Malkuth, the treatment is either one of assisting the free flow of force, or else supplementing the deficiency by the natural forces of nature, sunlight and ray therapy, both being beneficial.

But the condition is often first brought about by the emotional level, and then you must treat the Centre in the world of emotion. It is in this sphere of emotion, the astral plane, the sphere of magic, that much can be done by magical means in operations on this level.

7.
THE ETHERIC DOUBLE

The Etheric Centres

The Etheric Double makes contact with the physical body at the Centres on the Middle Pillar. At these Centres etheric energy discharges into the nervous system. The energy is all one; it is the Centre through which it discharges that determines its type.

This energy is an alternating current. It comes down from Kether and passes through Malkuth to the earth, and it comes up from the earth and passes through Kether to the Cosmic Kether. By concentrating the attention on a given Centre exclusively, the current can be checked and held there as by a dam, thus gathering a big head of power. It can then be projected objectively by the appropriate means.

If held in Kether, it produces the higher trance conditions or cosmic consciousness;

if held in Daath it yields magical power;

in Tiphareth emotional magnetism;

in Yesod sex magnetism;

in Malkuth basic energy, important in healing and recuperation.

It is only safe to use this method when the triangles representing the Individuality and the Personality form the Six-pointed Star; that is to say, when the Higher and Lower Selves are unified.

The rising current is of the same polarity as the lower triangle and therefore reinforces its voltage; but being of the opposite polarity to the higher triangle, is neutralised by it,

Principles of Esoteric Healing

and vice versa. When the Triangles form the Six-pointed Star, only the upper and lower points are disengaged. Consequently only in Malkuth and Kether are the forces free to act. On the other levels they are in equilibrium and stabilised by the opposite polarity. In the female, Malkuth is negative and Kether positive, and the position is reversed in the male.

The energy can either be drawn up on the form side of things, (magically), or drawn down on the consciousness side (mystically). The upwardly drawn Elemental energy stabilises the Sephirah in which it is functioning. The drawn down Spiritual energy is used for projection, being conditioned by the Centre through which it is projected.

Should the balance between the two energies not be maintained, the Centre is liable to injury. If the Elemental force does not reinforce the Centre sufficiently, the concentration of Spiritual force will burn it out and a "nervous breakdown" will take place.

If the Elemental force is brought up, and the counter-balancing Spiritual force is not brought down, the Elemental force will accumulate in the Centre until it bursts it. For a short time the Centre will function with great power and energy and then wear out, and the thin walls will allow the escape of magnetic force from the Etheric Double into the physical nervous system.

The physical energy will burn with a forced draught for a short time and then the brain and nervous tissue will begin to wear out; the subject will have recourse to stimulants, or, if possessed of the necessary knowledge, may draw upon the energy of another individual or group of individuals temporarily, thus delaying the final collapse.

Examples of these processes can be seen among psychics and occultists. The commonest cause of such an occurence is the over-hasty development of a Centre, which brings down

The Etheric Double

the projecting Spiritual force before the Elemental force has had time to build up the Centre. Another cause is an ascetic ideal which calls down the spiritual force and refuses to allow the Elemental force to rise to meet it.

The trouble may also occur if too much force is retained in the Centre for the development of the aura instead of being used for projection, which is the normal purpose of this operation. This purpose is legitimate up to a point, but if carried beyond that point, the strain may prove too much for the Centre and it will be damaged.

Death supervenes swiftly upon the destruction of a Centre, but sometimes the other Centres up and down the Middle Pillar are also damaged because of the upset of the equilibrium of the forces in them owing to the disorganisation of the adjacent Centre, which ceases to transmit as it should.

When the subject reincarnates, the injury in the Etheric Double will be reproduced, with consequent anomalies in the physical body. It may take several incarnations before the etheric structure returns to normal if the damage has been severe, and many obscure diseases owe their origin to this cause. There is no absolute cure, though the condition can be amelioriated. There are several forms of this disease, and when the Brow Centre is burnt out, it gives rise to Epilepsy.

Etheric disease or malfunction is hereditary for several generations on the physical plane because the Etheric Double is closely connected with the endocrine system, and any endocrine malfunction in the parent will affect the endocrine development of the child. The condition is mitigated at each remove, whether by direct physical heredity or by reincarnation, till it reaches a state of dilution when it will only declare itself under stress, and might pass unnoticed for the whole course of a tranquil life, only, however, to reappear unexpectedly if a descendant is placed under stress or there is intermarriage with a person of similar propensities.

Principles of Esoteric Healing

According to karmic law, persons with a tendency to a particular type of pathology tend to be born into families in which such pathology is hereditary, thus the spread of the condition through the race is limited. For the same reason, persons with etheric anomalies tend to marry persons with etheric anomalies, and let it be remembered that an etheric anomaly does not necessarily, or even commonly, take the same form in subsequent generations or incarnations, because the glands act as controls one to another, and if a gland is faulty from the moment of conception, its defects will influence the development of the gland it controls; thus the outward appearance of the anomaly may change completely though the underlying cause remains the same.

Each type of etheric anomaly will have a corresponding psycho-pathology, because the different Centres on the Tree govern the different levels of consciousness.

The Etheric Double and the Endocrine Glands

The Etheric Double may be defined as the Body of Energy. It consists of:

1. a Primary Circuit to the left and right of the spinal column;
2. a Secondary Circuit to the back and front of the aura;
3. the field of magnetic induction between them.

Contact between the Etheric Double and the physical body is:

1. along the pole of the spine, whence the central nervous system is supplied with the energy necessary for its functioning;
2. between the Etheric Centres and the endocrine glands.

The Etheric Double

The Ductless or Endocrine Glands control the chemistry of the blood, which is modified by the balance of their secretions. Alter the balance of the secretions and you alter the composition of the blood.

The composition of the blood determines the general metabolism which supplies the energy with which the physical body has to perform its functions. It also affects the irritability, or degree of response to stimulus, of the tissues; and the conductivity of the nerve fibres, lowering or increasing their resistance as the case may be.

The functioning of an incarnate being depends firstly upon:

1. adequate supplies of the factors necessary for metabolism;

2. the absence of factors (poisons) which alter the chemistry of the metabolic processes;

3. the mechanical intactness of the physical body;

4. absence of interference with the mechanical functioning of the body by heat, cold, or pressure beyond its power of adaptation.

The conduct of the vital processes depends equally upon a second set of factors which are connected with the Etheric Double:

1. the primary and secondary energy circuits already indicated. These derive their energy from the magnetic relationship between the mass of the Earth and the magnetic field of the Solar System, a continually fluctuating sphere of energy;

2. the set of Centres upon the Middle Pillar, and their relative development and intactness due to the conditions under which they functioned in previous incarnations;

3. the amount of vital energy directed into a given Centre at a given moment by the mind.

149

Principles of Esoteric Healing

In the average person this vital energy is regulated automatically by the subconscious mind and depends:

1. on the set of astral thought forms or memories brought over from the last life, which determines the degree of attention, inhibition, and reaction capacity of the aspects of consciousness associated with each Centre;

2. on the opening of the "valves" between Centre and gland due to the stimulating or inhibiting of the activity of the gland by the chemical composition of the nervous tissues of the gland itself.

In the more highly evolved person, in whom consciousness is taking over control from subconsciousness, control of the Centres, and in consequence of the glands associated with them, is achieved by the voluntary direction of attention to a particular Centre, or the voluntary withdrawal of attention therefrom. This is effected by dwelling in imagination on the images associated with the functions of the gland it is desired to stimulate, or upon the images associated with the functions of the Centre which acts as an inhibitor to the gland whose function it is desired to repress.

Medical research has revealed the factors dependant upon the organic integrity of the different glands. Let it never be forgotten, however, that the glandular system acts as a team, not individually. Each one, in addition to contributing to its own factor to the general metabolism and tone of the body and its parts, also contributes a factor which controls the functioning of its next of kin.

The relationship of the glands can be deduced from the sequence of their evolutionary development. It is a mistake to think that the situation of the spinal column determines the seniority of a gland. The original form of life was spherical. All the vital processes are implicit in the protoplasm of the early spherical forms. Note their order of emergence as

The Etheric Double

specialised organs and you will know the hierarchical arrangement of the glandular system.

It is important to know this, because as each gland develops, and in the degree of its development, it modifies the concord of its predecessors. Its secretion affects them, but their secretion does not affect it save through the influence of the general metabolism and tissue tone of the body in which it shares.

This is readily seen if we consider the relationship of the latest developed gland, the gonad, to the rest of the glandular concert. Let it be noted that, long and eagerly as mankind has sought it, there is no specific aphrodisiac; all the substances claiming that virtue act either through auto-suggestion, or through the general improvement in bodily tone, or through an increased irritability of the nervous system. On the other hand, the internal secretion of the gonad affects the functioning of every other gland in the body, with the subsequent control of all functioning.

In the practice of glandular therapy, remember that the gonad is the master gland. In the practice of psychotherapy, remember that it is under the immediate control of the mind. Remember the mind does not affect the body by direct action, nor the body the mind. Interaction always takes place through the intermediary of the glandular system and the Etheric Double. The relative predominance of the factors varies, but neither is totally absent, for they are sections in a circuit.

Functional endocrine disorder may produce changes in tissue tone, in metabolism, or in emotional and mental states, according to which gland is primarily concerned. Such functional disorders are due to the following causes:

1. Exhaustion of the gland due to the strain thrown on it by an acute febrile infection, hence the debility of convalesence;

Principles of Esoteric Healing

2. Exhaustion of the gland by excessive demands made upon it by the stresses of life;

3. Starvation of a gland by the inhibition of its due supply of energy from the Etheric Double, due to an emotional attitude or fixed idea. For an illustration of this, note the absence of youthfulness, mental and physical, in the sexually repressed.

The diagnosis of (1) is a simple matter, dependant on the physical history. The distinction between (2) and (3) depends on the proper taking of a psychological history, and needs to be carefully made; for (3) can set up stresses which can lead to (2), or (2) may be due conditions which lead to (3), and the distinction has to be carefully drawn and the originating factor determined, for the treatment depends on the distinction.

In breaking a vicious circle, deal if possible with the entire circuit. That is to say, when mind and body are interacting and reinforcing each other in the production of a condition, deal with them both in treatment so that they again reinforce each other in the curative effort. An improved physical condition will produce a sense of well being which reacts on the mind; and the improved mental state gives positive autosuggestion to the body. Moreover, a mind thus invigorated will open itself to, and reach out towards, those objective vital forces so little understood at the present day.

Endocrine Malfunction

There are four types of Endocrine malfunction:
1. Congenital;
2. Developmental;
3. Functional;
4. Menopausal.

The Etheric Double

Congenital

This type of glandular malfunction concerns those disorders arising in a previous incarnation. These result in organic defects of the ductless glands and central nervous system developing during the pre-natal life and declaring themselves in due course. If the degree of the defect is not too severe, a considerable amount of adaptation can often be secured, but the individual will never be of standard pattern nor able to endure adequately the stresses of life, and will need to lead a sheltered existence.

Such persons, however, may be socially valuable by reason of their defects, which rendering them abnormally responsive to stimuli of different types, advantage them in certain ways while handicapping them in others. Of such are the seers and visionaries.

Let it be remembered that departure from the standard pattern of humanity is compatible with a healthy and harmonious life, provided circumstances can be adjusted to accommodate it. The shoe must fit the foot. Society, however, requires the foot to fit the shoe. This is the key to many functional disorders, or more strictly speaking, disorders that were originally functional but, interfering with development, resulted in deformity.

Such a deformity, however, will not carry over into another incarnation, being physical. It is the etheric deformities that appear as congenital malformations in subsequent lives. Physical conditions do not affect the Etheric Double, save by inhibiting the circulation of magnetism by increasing the resistance of the nervous tissues.

This type of endocrine defect we will call Congenital, remembering that congenital conditions always originate in previous lives unless there is some serious interference with the nutrition of the mother during gestation.

Principles of Esoteric Healing

Developmental

Emotional stresses due to maladaptation can distort the development of the immature individual. This may be due to an abnormally sensitive individual being unable to accommodate himself to the stresses of life, or to an abnormally stressful life making undue demands on the individual. The result is faulty endocrine habit in after life, partly due to the chronic reduction of the blood supply to the gland through inhibition of its function, and partly due to the exhaustion of another gland through over-stimulation of its function. Unbalanced glandular function leads to emotional unbalance and defects of attention and concentration, to metabolic disturbances and changes in tissue tone in all the systems of the body, as has already been pointed out.

A person in whom developmental endocrine imbalance supervenes will never be a normal individual, but he can become a healthy and useful, or even valuable one, as the history of genius shows. Indeed, it might be said that genius depends to some degree on endocrine imbalance, which permits of an intensive concentration of energy at a given Centre, even at the cost of the others, which never occurs in a well balanced individual.

Functional

This type of endocrine disorder is due to the inhibition or over-stimulation of function of a ductless gland by subjective psychological causes after a normal maturity has been reached. Such drastic interference with Nature may be due either to the ethical concepts or conventional inhibitions of the individual, or the need to make adaptations to circumstances not under his control.

Such types of disorder respond well to psychological treatment of the re-educational variety. A new outlook can be

The Etheric Double

gained, or a compromise found with the aid of wise psychological guidance, provided the psychologist has the sense to approach the problem from the viewpoint of the patient.

This type of disorder declares itself soon after maturity is reached, and the glands are transmitting etheric forces for which there is no outlet, thus giving rise to magnetic and consequently emotional congestion. This is the true functional endocrine disorder.

Menopausal

This form of endocrine malfunction occurs at "the change of life" in both men and women, when readjustments of endocrine balance and function normally take place. If severe stresses have occurred during adolescence and maturity, an exhaustion of glandular tissue may supervene at this juncture and require treatment by the appropriate substitution therapy. If repression of function has done violence to nature, subconsciously motivated reactions may take place in a last desperate effort to secure fulfilment of the life purposes before it is too late. A wise compounding of psychology and sedatives is here indicated while glandular adjustments are in process, until the individual settles down to the contentment of the slower rhythms of old age.

Let it be remembered, however, that the endocrine glands are the organs of adjustment to environment, and that their functioning is not fixed but fluctuating, like a pressure gauge. That there is a limit to their range of adaptation, and that if the demands made on them exceed that limit, their response will fail to secure accommodation and disaster will ensue. Adaptation cannot be counselled as a matter of course; rebellion is sometimes indicated.

It is well known that often the change in life is blamed for everything of which the patient can complain, and especially

Principles of Esoteric Healing

those of a psychologically unbalanced and unstable personality are very likely to have greater upsets at such times. It is mostly their mental and emotional attitude to life which has a deleterious effect upon the normal functioning of their glands, and so disturbs them especially; whereas the woman of harmonious and balanced life passes through such phases gradually and without disturbance. It is always a time of stress and change, and proper and harmonious adaptation of the various glands to the altered rhythm and demand upon them does not always happen. Hormone therapy is of great benefit in these cases.

Principles concerning Conception and Birth

From the point of view of the Higher Self, birth is an entering into incarnation for it, and death is when it is released from the lessons and bondage of form to return to its own plane and absorb its experiences.

There is a saying that the soul comes through the father. In other words, that it is the masculine or positive principle that gives the stimulus which brings in the new life. It is the feminine principle which is required to give birth thereto.

Concerning conception, the Higher Self comes down and becomes drawn towards the Earth at the time that fertilisation of the ovum occurs. From the etheric point of view, there is a unit of negative and positive force which, on fusion, forms a temporary neutral field. The contact does not actually take place at the time of intercourse, as that does not necessarily bear any immediate relationship to the actual moment of conception, which is the time of fertilisation of the ovum.

The Higher Self of the incarnating Ego does not completely overshadow at this stage, but it has a rapport with the fertilised ovum. With the development of the ovum and the

The Etheric Double

growth of the foetus, this rapport becomes stronger — but it is as yet only a rapport and not a very intimate one.

Quickening signifies that the mother appreciates the foetal movements for the first time, and this occurs, as a rule, at the end of the seventeenth week. In popular belief this occurrence is said to be the time when the soul is present. There is some esoteric foundation for this belief, as the Individuality does take a closer grip upon its future vehicle at this stage; and through birth and early childhood the Higher Self gradually comes into closer union. The process becomes somewhat different later on for the once-born and the twice-born.

The incarnating soul will be in a body suitable to express the karma brought over from the past. Therefore, the type of etheric body which it will have in this life, based on the type of physical body it inherits from its parents, will be a very close parallel to the type of etheric body which the influence of the Ghost would have built. There is, therefore, a parallel, but not necessarily an exact one. The physical heredity is fixed and subject only to future changes from modifying factors such as environment, nutrition, or the life that will be led on the physical plane.

Apart from those physical factors which do influence the etheric body according to the health or otherwise of the physical body, there will also be the subconscious influence of the Ghost working upon the etheric body. This influence will tend to modify the etheric body towards its own pattern. As the person grows older, this influence, by altering the etheric pattern, particularly of the chakras, will become relatively stronger.

The sphere of attraction between the relative neutral condition of the fertilised ovum and the incarnating entity is a question really of vibratory keynotes. There are Higher Selves who wish to incarnate for experience and there are so many fertilised ova to which they could go, but the one which is

Principles of Esoteric Healing

suitable to their own condition will be at a certain rate of vibration. A Higher Self could have an attraction towards that which will be the means of giving it further experience, in a similar fashion to the attraction between two people in a group of strangers.

The Ghost and the aura of the mother have an influence in causing foetal abnormalities when the origin is not physical. When the result is a stillbirth the incarnating Ego has a short experience of incarnation in the flesh although it has not lived as a separate being.

Astrological Factors

The soul of a being comes into incarnation when the conditions in the psychic atmosphere match its own psychic make-up. When the key fits the lock, the door opens.

Remember, in this connection, that time on the inner planes is a mode of consciousness, and in no way bound to the revolutions of the planet Earth, and, therefore, cannot be measured by them.

The door opens when the key fits the lock; the soul comes into incarnation when its conditions and Earth conditions are in alignment — I speak metaphorically. It is incorrect to think that the psychic atmosphere prevailing at the place and time of birth have any effect on the incoming soul, for the soul's condition is determined by karma. But because the soul and the psychic conditions of that soul at that time and place are identical, it is possible to deduce the condition of the soul, and its karma, by studying the figure of the heavens as seen from the place of birth at the birth hour.

Because the body of the Earth insulates the surface from all influences below the horizon, according to the temperament of make-up of a person will be his reactions to the ever-changing psychic influence of the Earth's atmosphere.

The Etheric Double

But remember this, in seeking to draw conclusions from astrological data, that persons vary in degree of development, and their reactions differ accordingly. Therefore the Qabalists talk of the Four Worlds of Manifestation and the four bodies of man functioning in their respective worlds. According to the world where is a man's focus of being so will his reactions be to the planetary influences.

That is the true basis of astrology. It is the science of the calculation of the psychic influences and conditions of the Solar System. Mankind are influenced by these conditions in proportion to their degree of development.

Man is the microcosm of the Macrocosm. Every factor or ingredient in his being is derived from a corresponding factor in the Macrocosm. The Macrocosm, for practical purposes, save in the very highly evolved, may be taken to be limited to the Solar System. The constellations of the Zodiac do not represent sources of influence directed towards the planet of Earth, as the geocentric astrology conceived, but act as markers for the rays of influence radiating from the Sun, through which the Earth passes in its annual orbit.

The Sun is the source of all energy in the Solar System even as it is the source of all substance, for the planets are condensed from the nebula which was the Sun. Different phases of evolution took place on the different planets; each planet, therefore, acquired a particular temperament, and radiates that influence with its light.

The influence radiated by a planet is modified by the place it occupies in its orbit, because it is then subjected to the Ray influences from the Sun, which is known by the name of the constellation towards which it is directed. This is the esoteric key to astrology.

The nearer a planet is to its zenith the greater is its influence but the influence of the planets is affected according to the plane on which a man's life is focussed.

Principles of Esoteric Healing

If he is of the earth, earthy, he will react like an animal, his destiny is the destiny of the race. If centred on the higher astral plane, he is extremely susceptible to planetary influences. If he is centred on the mental plane he is sensitive to them but able to dominate them. If centred on the spiritual he will be immune. In the proportion of these factors he will rule his stars or be ruled by them. The mental with psychic awareness will control. The purely material are relatively insensitive except racially and as their physiological processes respond to the magnetic tides within the Solar System.

Astrology as a method of prognostication in general is highly unreliable. As a means of providing matters to be taken into account it is extremely useful, for it frequently supplies the resolution of the unknown factors in a situation. It tells you what are the subtle influences. If a person's exact birth moment is known his reactions can be calculated, provided his degree of development has been correctly evaluated. The only person who can estimate that is his Initiator.

Astrology therefore is a sacred science in the strict sense of the word and can be used rightly by initiates only. In the hands of the uninitiated it is a very uncertain tool.

INDEX

A. G. Tansley F. R. S., 8
Higher Self, 6, 21-23, 27,
  51, 69-70, 74, 90,
  119-121, 130, 135-
  136, 139, 156-158
Anatomy, 5, 27-28, 78
Animals, 76
Apollo, 101, 103-104, 110
Art of Healing, 5, 17
Asclepios, 101, 103-104,
  110
Asclepios Apollo, 101, 104
Astral, 5, 9, 21, 32-33, 39-
  40, 43, 46, 48-53,
  71-74, 103-105, 108-
  109, 115-116, 119,
  121-122, 124, 142,
  144, 150, 160
Astral Plane, 5, 9, 32, 40,
  49-50, 52, 74, 116,
  124, 160
Astral World, 142
Astrological Factors, 6,
  158
Astrology, 5, 32-35, 159-
  160
Aura, 68, 71-74, 93, 105,
  109-110, 138, 141,
  147-148, 158
Binah, 94
Birth, 6, 29-30, 156-158,
  160
Body of Energy, 148
Brow Centre, 117-119,
  130, 147
Budapest, 11
Caduceus, 116-117
Carstairs, 10-11
Celestial Surgeon, 110

Central Pillar, 53, 78, 87,
  113, 115, 117-118,
  120-121, 123-124,
  128, 133, 139-140
Central Sephiroth, 140
Centre of Daath, 128
Centre of Hod, 87
Centre of Malkut, 128
Centre of Malkuth, 134
Chesed, 54, 113, 115, 120
Child, 55, 75, 79, 139, 147
Childhood, 132, 135, 157
Christ, 106
Christian Science, 84
Clairvoyance, 70
Clairvoyant Faculty, 6, 66,
  70
Classification of Disease,
  43, 45, 47, 49, 51,
  53, 55, 57, 59
Conception, 6, 29, 148,
  156
Consciousness, 10, 13, 21-
  22, 25, 27-28, 30, 38,
  46, 48, 61-64, 67, 71,
  73-74, 77, 80, 88, 91,
  93, 95, 98, 124, 134,
  138, 140, 144-146,
  148, 150, 158
Correspondences, 6, 33,
  35, 38, 49, 75, 77,
  121
Cosmic Doctrine, 10, 62,
  95
Cosmic Fire, 62
Cosmic Law, 27, 32, 41,
  52, 58
Cosmic Plane, 27
Cosmos, 18, 28, 37, 41, 51,

  113
Crown Centre, 115, 117,
  134
Crucified One, 139
Daath, 54, 71, 77, 93-94,
  115, 117-119, 128,
  130, 145
Death, 13, 15, 57, 86, 95,
  147, 156
Diagnosis, 5-6, 12, 22, 39,
  41, 54, 61-63, 65-69,
  74, 77, 101, 119,
  134-136, 139-141,
  152
Diathesis, 6, 92-93
Dion Fortune, 4-5, 7-10,
  12-15, 62
Disease, 5, 9, 11, 18, 23,
  27, 29, 32, 42-43,
  45-47, 49-53, 55, 57-
  59, 63, 69, 72, 75-78,
  81, 83-84, 86, 90,
  92-93, 95-97, 119,
  122, 137, 147
Diseases, 5, 8, 35, 41-46,
  48-49, 51, 53, 55-56,
  58-59, 72, 74, 78, 83,
  86, 90, 92, 122, 137,
  147
Disharmony, 14, 18, 22,
  41, 44, 52, 74, 76-77,
  84, 86, 137, 140, 143
Disturbance, 42, 48, 92-93,
  119, 137, 142, 156
Divagations, 41, 44
Divine Spark, 27, 62-63,
  118, 142
Dr. Evans, 10, 12
Dr. Ignez Semmelwiess, 11

161

Principles of Esoteric Healing

Dr. Taverner, 8, 12

Dr. Theodore Moriarty, 8

Dr. Thomas Penry Evans, 8

Earth Spirit, 40

East, 103

Ego, 30, 91-92, 156, 158

Elementals, 72, 104

Elements, 15, 36-38, 123, 125, 133

Emotional World, 117-118, 120, 128-129, 137

Emotional World of Daath, 118

Endocrine, 6, 9, 51, 53, 79, 91-92, 118, 120-121, 125, 144, 147-149, 151-155

Endocrine Glands, 6, 120-121, 148-149, 155

Endocrine Malfunction, 6, 147, 152, 155

Epidaurus, 102

Epilepsy, 74, 78, 147

Esoteric Hygiene, 6, 110

Esoteric Medicine, 7, 10, 12-13, 18, 25, 32, 41, 91, 110

Esoteric Therapeutics, 7, 13

Essential Self, 142

Etheric, 5-6, 9, 14-15, 30, 36, 39, 43-44, 46-50, 52-53, 59, 71-72, 76-78, 87, 93, 100-105, 110, 112, 115-116, 119-120, 124-128, 131, 133, 135, 138, 144-149, 151-153, 155-157, 159

Etheric Centres, 6, 14, 145, 148

Etheric Double, 5-6, 30, 46-49, 71-72, 93, 145-149, 151-153

Etheric Leakage, 6, 103

Etheric World, 133, 144

Excretion, 77, 93

Exhaustion, 151-152, 154-155

Extrovert, 37

Fat, 31

Fate, 28-30

Fatigue, 50, 89, 99-100

Fear, 50, 106

Fire, 55, 62, 97, 125

Fire of God, 62

Fortune, 4-5, 7-15, 19, 35, 62

Four Elements, 36-37, 123, 125, 133

Four Levels, 12, 80, 113, 135

Four Types, 36-37, 121, 152

Four Worlds, 6, 54, 102, 113, 115, 117, 122, 125, 128, 133-134, 138-140, 159

Four Worlds of Manifestation, 159

Ghost, 5, 28-32, 48, 76, 119, 126, 157-158

Golden Age of Greece, 102

Golden Dawn, 9

Greece, 81, 102, 104

Greek Temple of Healing, 101

Green Ray, 118, 140

Group Soul, 57, 66

Harmony, 21, 32, 41, 48, 52, 80, 84, 102, 135

Healer Priest, 21, 66, 70

Healing, 4-5, 7, 12, 14, 17, 20-24, 32, 41, 44, 48, 51, 59, 65, 69, 79, 81-85, 90, 99, 101-105, 109-110, 119, 134, 139, 144-145

Healing Temple, 110

Heart, 24, 55, 63, 71, 91, 115, 119, 121-123, 125, 130

Heart Centre, 115, 119, 121-123, 125, 130

Heaven, 134

Hermetic Order, 9

Higher Selves, 90, 157

Hod, 87, 113, 115, 124, 127, 139, 141

Holy Sephiroth, 93

Homeopathy, 98

Hygeia, 103

Hygieia, 103-104

Hypnosis, 6, 85-86, 88-89

Hypnotism, 86, 88-89

Individuality, 27-29, 32, 145, 157

Infection, 46, 55, 58, 93, 108, 111, 151

Initiator, 160

Inner Light, 4, 7, 15, 166

Inner Planes, 66, 89-90, 158

Insanity, 45, 48

Insomnia, 6, 98-100, 118

Introvert, 37

Intuition, 19, 64, 69, 128, 136

Irritability, 55, 149, 151

Jesus, 106, 108

Kether, 93-94, 115-118, 121-122, 125, 132-133, 145-146

King, 139

Kundalini, 128, 131

Light of Evolution, 5, 27

Likeness of God, 28

Logos, 112

London, 7-8, 166

Lower Self, 90, 135

Lower Selves, 69, 145

Luna, 36

162

Index

Lunar, 132
Macrocosm, 35, 41, 113, 134, 159
Maiya Curtis-Webb, 9
Maiya Tranchell-Hayes, 9
Margaret Lumley Brown, 15
Marriage, 10, 50
Mars, 33, 35, 47, 141
Master Jesus, 108
Master of Masters, 106
Master of Medicine, 5, 7, 9-12
Material World, 118, 120-123, 129, 133, 144
Maternity Clinic, 11
Meditation, 6, 17-18, 25, 61, 65, 67, 70, 80, 101-104
Mediterranean, 102
Mental Body, 33, 123
Mental Level, 38, 52-54, 77, 99, 115, 118, 122, 124, 127-129, 140, 142
Mental Plane, 5, 52-53, 160
Mental World, 54, 117-118, 120-121, 127-129, 137, 140
Mercury, 33
Mercy, 140
Microcosmic Sephiroth, 113
Microcosmic Tree of Life, 77
Middle Pillar, 145, 147, 149
Moon, 35-36, 47, 53, 93, 132
Netzach, 87, 113, 115, 124, 127, 141
New Age, 23
North, 103, 108

Obsession, 45-46, 74, 103, 105-107
Occult, 8-10, 12, 25, 33, 74, 117-119, 131
Omega Temple, 9
Orthodox, 10, 18-20, 25, 40, 92
Overshadowing, 6, 32, 105, 107-108
Pairs of Opposites, 140
Paracelsus, 121
Paracelsus, 11
Pasteur, 11
Path of Evolution, 62
Pathologies, 54, 115, 117, 125, 128-131, 133, 142
Paths, 15, 113, 141
Pelvic Centre, 113, 120, 128-130
Personality, 22, 28-29, 32, 58, 63, 70, 75-76, 100, 118, 120-121, 124-125, 132-133, 135, 139, 144-145, 156
Perversions, 130
Pest, 11
Phlegmatic, 37-38
Pillar, 53, 78, 87, 113, 115, 117-118, 120-121, 123-124, 128, 133, 139-140, 145, 147, 149
Pillar of Force, 140
Pillars, 54, 87, 103, 139-141
Pineal Centre, 69, 71, 73, 112, 115
Poison, 55-57
Poisoning, 5, 42, 56-57
Potencies, 36, 39, 47, 138, 141
Potency, 47, 104-105, 138

Power, 34, 40, 47, 51, 66, 68, 70, 74-75, 82-83, 85, 87, 89, 104-105, 110, 131, 135, 140, 143, 145-146, 149
Priestess, 66
Primary Circuit, 148
Pythoness, 15
Qabalah, 14
Qabalists, 159
Qlippothic, 108
Rapports, 6, 12, 72, 101, 105, 126, 131
Ray, 27, 47, 73, 118, 140, 159
Rays, 47, 61, 63, 159
Relaxation, 6, 79-80, 100
Renaissance, 11
Reproduction, 93
Rings, 61
Root Centre, 113, 123-124, 129-130, 132-134
Royal Magazine, 8
Saprophytes, 57
Saturn, 35
Science, 10, 12, 17, 19-20, 24-25, 28, 33, 35, 39, 41, 44, 62-63, 65, 84, 92, 159-160
Secondary Circuit, 148
Seed Atoms, 29
Semmelweis, 11
Sephirah Hod, 139
Sephirah Yesod, 128
Sephiroth, 15, 53-54, 93-94, 101, 113, 131, 138-140
Sepsis, 5, 55, 57-58, 131
Side Pillars, 54, 87, 139-141
Solar Plexus, 69, 94, 111-112, 115, 124-126
Solar System, 28, 35, 41, 149, 159-160

163

Principles of Esoteric Healing

Spirit, 15, 20, 27, 38-40, 42, 61, 75-76, 115, 117, 128, 142, 144
Spiritual Healers, 23
Spiritual Plane, 52, 84, 103, 140
Spiritual Sun of Kether, 125
Spiritual World, 118, 120-121, 124, 128, 140
Spiritualist, 10
Spleen Centre, 124-126
Starvation, 49, 121, 152
Subtle Bodies, 5, 27, 30-32, 36, 42, 48, 105, 110, 112
Suggestion, 6, 9, 34, 81-83, 85
Sun, 4, 28, 47, 49, 93, 102, 125, 159
Supernal Sephiroth, 15
Supernal Triangle, 117
Temple, 6, 9, 12, 15, 81, 101-103, 109-110
Temple Sleep, 81, 101
The Airy or Mental, 40
The Brow Centre, 117-119, 130, 147
Throat, 56, 115, 120
Throat Centre, 115, 120
Tiphareth, 54, 94, 113, 115, 121, 124-125, 130, 138-139, 145
Treatment, 6, 14, 18, 21, 23, 37, 39-40, 42-43, 45, 47, 54, 61, 63, 81, 83, 86-87, 90, 95-96, 99-101, 103-105, 109, 119, 122, 132, 135-136, 139-140, 142, 144, 152, 154-155
Tree of Life, 14, 53, 71, 77-78, 87, 100, 113
Triangles, 145-146

Tuberculosis, 59
Universe, 5, 28, 34, 41, 49
Unmanifest, 62
Unseen, 23-24
Venus, 33, 35, 47
Visualisation, 70-71, 101-102, 122-123
Vitality, 6, 23, 40, 45, 50, 52, 58, 72, 87-88, 91, 93, 96, 112, 118, 122, 124, 129, 135, 137-138
Water, 38
Western Mystery Tradition, 70
Western Tradition, 36
White, 47, 102-104, 111
World of Assiah, 144
World of Atziluth, 140
World of Briah, 140
World of Spirit, 115
Worlds, 6, 23, 54, 102, 113, 115, 117-118, 122, 125, 128, 133-134, 137-140, 159
Worlds of Daath, 118
Yesod, 94, 113, 120, 124, 128, 130, 132, 141, 145
Ypres, 10
Zodiac, 159

THE SOCIETY OF THE INNER LIGHT

The Society of the Inner Light publishes a quarterly Journal, to which Gareth Knight has contributed. The Society also offers an Unsupervised Study Course to ex-UK residents and a Supervised Course to people living in the United Kingdom. For further details of the Journal or Study courses please write to:

The Secretariat
Society of the Inner Light
38 Steele's Road
London NW3 4RG
Great Britain

The Society has a web site:
www.innerlight.org.uk
and an e-mail address:
sil@innerlight.org.uk

Principles of Esoteric Healing

MARTIN PRECHTEL
- shaman Guatnmala -